VARIETY

in your preaching

VARIETY
in your preaching

Faris D. Whitesell
Northern Baptist Seminary

Lloyd M. Perry
Gordon Divinity School

Fleming H. Revell Company
Old Tappan, New Jersey

Printed in the United States of America

To

Cynthia Ann Whitesell
Rixson Merle Perry
Gregg Chandler Perry

Contents

Foreword

No field offers a greater challenge and opportunity to those who enter it than the Christian ministry. Success in such work is directly related to the effectiveness of the preacher in the pulpit. Today, more than ever before, his sermons must be the means of strong religious leadership in his congregation, his community, and his country. The voice of the Church must be heard above the voices of the many materialistic and commercial agencies which, from the platform, and over the radio and television, seek to influence the lives of men.

Therefore the training given potential Christian ministers is of greatest importance. It should inspire them not only to dedicate their lives completely and courageously; to learn facts, principles, and theology; but it should develop in them the highest degree of skill in preaching. To this end, intensive, sound training in speech must be *combined* with that in homiletics in a program of instruction to insure sermons which are carefully planned and effectively presented. No part of this program should be left to the inspiration of the moment or chance.

The authors of *Variety in Your Preaching* have taken an important forward step with the publication of this volume. They have combined these necessary materials in teachable form for the seminary; they have provided a source of practical help for the minister in the pulpit. The chapters which follow are organized and written to train men to preach more articulately, more impressively, and more convincingly, the messages so vital to Christian leadership in our time.

Evanston, Illinois,
March 7, 1953

Karl F. Robinson
Chairman, Department of
Speech Education
Northwestern University.

Introduction

Variety is an insistent demand of our times. We live in a rapid, restless, changing world. Variety is evident on every hand in the world of men and affairs. Personalities differ, styles vary, habits and modes of life change. We relish variety in our food, our reading, our places of travel, our personal contacts, our patterns of activity.

Variety adds zest to life. As the old proverb says, "Variety is the spice of life." A world of unchanging sameness would be deadening. God's example in nature is one of variety. Infinite diversity pervades the animal kingdom, the plant kingdom, the mineral kingdom and the starry hosts above. No two blades of grass are alike, no two leaves, no two snowflakes, no two people. If our creativity follows the divine pattern, it will reveal wide variation. The monotonous assembly line of mass production may be prevalent in our mechanized age, but it does not follow God's method.

Since preachers are dwelling with varied human beings, in every type of environment, we would naturally think that variation would be desirable in preaching, and the authors believe that it is. Preaching is the most important task that God commits to men, in that not only the issues of time but those of eternity depend on its impact. Therefore, the preacher should seek to do his best in the pulpit.

The authors hold firmly that all preaching should be Biblical—the Word of God its fountain source—and that it should exalt Christ in such a way that men will come to trust Him, know Him, love Him, and yield their lives to Him.

The philosophy and aim of this book, then, is to emphasize the importance of preaching the Word of God by a wide variety of methods and emphases, thus providing an attractive, appetizing and balanced diet of spiritual food. Holding as they do, that the Bible is the fully inspired and absolutely authoritative Word of God, "profitable for doctrine, for reproof, for correction, for instruction in righteousness, that the man of God may be perfect, thoroughly furnished unto every good work" (2 Tim. 3:16–17), they have sought to emphasize Biblical preaching as the one and only type worthy of the Christian pulpit.

Bible preaching is the most exciting venture men can undertake, but they must not conform it to a single mold, thus making it tedious and uninteresting. Knowing that certain preachers preach the whole counsel of God faithfully but follow an unchanging pattern; and that other men believe the whole Bible, and intend to preach it, but incline to emphasize only certain doctrines, books and passages, commonly called "hobbyriding," the authors seek to show the value of using all the emphases and parts of the Bible.

To preach to the same congregation from week

to week and year to year with interesting freshness and diversity is not easy. If the lay people begin to feel that they will hear the same old thing in the same old way, with only minor variations, Sunday after Sunday, attendance will decline and it will be time for the pastor to seek a new field or else awaken to the need for more variety in his homiletical work.

The chapters in this book seek to take the preacher step by step through an efficient and practical procedure of sermon making. While these steps may vary according to men and circumstances, yet, after considerable experience in sermon preparation and years of experience in teaching homiletics in the classroom, the authors believe that they have set forth herein the most efficient and time-saving methods of sermonizing. They would ask the reader to test these suggested steps and discover their practicality for himself. Therefore, the chapters in this book do not follow the usual order in homiletics books. For example, the chapter on introductions comes near the last, as, rightly, one cannot prepare an introduction properly until he has prepared the rest of the sermon and knows what he has to induce; and the chapter on aims comes first, since the aim should have priority in sermon preparation.

The preacher who seeks to put variety into his preaching will develop his own abilities. As he attempts new emphases, new methods and new approaches, he will discover unused areas to challenge his abilities; and he will find new capacities within himself not heretofore used.

Variety in preaching will add zest to preaching responsibilities, making them more lively and attractive. Variety in sermon construction will develop the preacher intellectually by forcing a broadening of the areas of his research; will tend to make him socially acceptable to all groups within the community; will help him to become economically secure in that his services will be in demand; will give him a clear conscience that he is adequately serving his God, his congregation and his community; thus he will experience a higher level of emotional stability and will be more spiritually alert and fruitful. The preacher will gain the benefits idealized in the basic philosophy of general theological education.

We all naturally tend to fall into habits, particularly bad ones. The preacher may become enmeshed in monotonous practices which hinder his effectiveness. The people are not likely to point out these handicaps to their pastor. In fact, they may not realize what is wrong beyond the fact that they are tired of their minister and his preaching. He no longer interests and challenges them. They know what truths, phraseology and methods of delivery to expect each time he stands up to declare the Gospel. They long to hear either a new voice or to have the old truths presented in new ways.

We are not advocating that the preacher should be a showman pulling new stunts out of his bag of tricks each time he preaches. Nor are we claiming that one must never do the same thing again and again. We insist only that the Gospel messenger should seek always to use variety within the bounds of propriety.

The philosophy of this book, therefore, is that Biblical preaching should be characterized by a wholesome variety which utilizes all modern rhetorical and homiletical possibilities to their maximum. The tested step-by-step procedure for attaining this ideal forms the content of this book.

Faris D. Whitesell
Lloyd M. Perry

VARIETY
in your preaching

I

Vary the Aims of Your Sermons

Every sermon should have an aim. What is the use of preaching unless there is an aim, goal or purpose? If you aim at nothing you will hit nothing. Yet we fear that many sermons are preached without proper aims; the preacher is merely fulfilling an assignment or performing a duty. No wonder he often fails.

Regarding the sermonic aim, John Hall, in the Yale lectures of 1875, wrote:

Have an aim in each sermon. Do not enter on it because you must preach something. If any one should say to you, What are you driving at? you should have no hesitation in answering. Let there be, for example, one great truth, of which you give the evidence, the elucidation, and the application, or one great duty of which you have the obligation and the best helps you can to its performance. Direct your arrows at objects without being personal; come near your hearers. Letters dropped into the post office without addresses go to the dead-letter office, and are of no use to anybody.[1]

And Nathanael J. Burton, in the same lectureship, for 1883–84, said:

[1] John Hall, *God's Word Through Preaching* (Willing and Williamson, Toronto, 1875), p. 115.

19

It has been the sin of my life that I have not always taken aim. I have been a lover of subjects. If I had loved men more and loved subjects only as God's instruments of good for men, it would have been better. . . .[2]

The need for varying the aim of sermons is easily apparent when we consider the differing attitudes of audiences the preacher has to face. Most of his audiences are *sympathetic*. They have gathered to hear a discussion of the Word of God and are ready to accept what the minister says, so long as it is in general conformity to the Scriptures. This is a believing audience from the standpoint of persuasion. The aim should be to dramatize the material presented.

Other audiences may be *apathetic*, or indifferent. They lack definite feeling toward the message or messenger. Here the purpose will be to use attention-getting material.

Sometimes an audience may be *hostile*, or antagonistic. The speaker should be careful to show respect to such an audience. He should approach it on the basis of common ground; or by the circuitous approach wherein illustrations are used which have no logical connection with the point at hand; or take the approach with statements with which the audience readily agrees, or the inductive approach, a series of particular incidents which lead up to the general statement of truth; or the frank approach, in which the speaker openly states his case and lets

---

[2] Nathanael J. Burton, *In Pulpit and Parish* (The Macmillan Company, New York, 1925), p. 53.

the decision rest on the intelligence and spirit of fair play of his audience.

Another audience may be *doubtful*. The demand here is for factual material. This involves employing the principles of general semantics.[3]

Aims may be classified as *general* and *specific*. The general aims inhere in the very nature and purpose of Christian preaching, for naturally the preacher's aims will differ somewhat from those of the secular speaker. The three aims we suggest are comprehensive and should always guide the preacher.

The first general aim is *to preach the Word of God*. Every pulpit effort should try to interpret the Word of God and apply it to human lives regardless of the occasion or the homiletical processes. Paul's solemn charge to Timothy should determine the general content of preaching:

I charge thee in the sight of God, and of Christ Jesus, who shall judge the living and the dead, and by his appearing and his kingdom: preach the word; be urgent in season, out of season; reprove, rebuke, exhort with all longsuffering and teaching (2 Tim. 4:1–2, ASV).

The next general aim should be *to preach in the power of the Holy Spirit*. Paul set the pattern in this respect when he wrote to the Thessalonians:

... Our gospel came not unto you in word only, but also in power, and in the Holy Spirit, and in much assurance. (1 Thes. 1:5, ASV).

3 See Irving J. Lee, *Language Habits in Human Affairs* (Harper & Brothers, New York, 1941).

Peter refers to apostolic preaching as having been done ". . . by them that have preached the gospel unto you with the Holy Ghost sent down from heaven . . ." (1 Pet. 1:12). Preaching in the energy of the flesh is fruitless preaching. Even as the Spirit of God brooded over the original creation, bringing order out of chaos, even so He can bring homiletical order out of the chaos of aimless sermonic construction.

The third general aim should be *to preach with homiletical skill.* The Spirit-empowered pulpiteer should know and use the tried and true principles of preaching wrought out in the laboratory of preaching experience down through the Christian centuries. Nor should he let himself fall below modern secular public-speaking theory. In sermon planning, preparation, construction and delivery he will seek to utilize all that both the fields of secular public speech and homiletics can offer him. Thus he will be a polished shaft in the Spirit's hands.

Before suggesting specific aims for the sermon, we may well ask what determines our aims? The answer to this question can be given broadly in three suggestions: *the Scriptures, the needs of the people,* and *the capacities of the preacher.* The Scriptures contain the standards of faith and practice to which the preacher should seek to bring his people. This is a lifetime task. He will likely find out what the needs of the people are as he moves among them.

Dr. A. W. Blackwood gives as a fourth suggestion the idea that the *state of the times* affects the substance and tone color of every sermon. If the people are lacking in Christian love, in missionary vision, or spiritual discernment, the preacher should gear his sermons to meet these needs. But no preacher can successfully aim beyond what he himself believes and practices.

Turning to *the specific aims,* we look first to secular public speaking. Quintilian said, "There are also three objects which an orator must accomplish: to inform, to move, to please."[4] Dr. George Glasgow of Northwestern University indicates five aims for public speaking: to inform, to inspire, to convince, to actuate and to entertain.[5] Professor Lionel Crocker of Dennison University gives a similar list of aims as: to entertain, to instruct, to actuate, to convince and to impress.[6] Preaching must include and go beyond these. The Roman Catholic writer, Thomas V. Liske, indicates four possible purposes for the priest as a speaker, namely, explaining, convincing, persuading and entertaining.[7] He further says:

The public speaker, especially the preacher, must be a keen-sighted archer aiming at the target of definite accomplishment in each speech. He must be a leader who brings his fellow travelers directly to a fixed destination without wandering down side paths.[8]

4 *Institutes of Oratory* (J. S. Watson translation, 1856), Book III, chap. 5, par. 1–2.
5 George M. Glasgow, *Dynamic Public Speaking* (Harper & Brothers, New York, 1950), p. 46.
6 Lionel Crocker, *Public Speaking for College Students* (American Book Company, New York, 1941), pp. 242–247.
7 Thomas V. Liske, *Effective Preaching* (The Macmillan Company, New York, 1951), pp. 117–119.
8 Thomas V. Liske, *idem.,* p. 116.

We recognize five specific aims in evangelical preaching. Every sermon should be governed by one or more of these aims. The first specific aim is *instruction*. People should know the Bible better, should understand the fundamental doctrines of the Christian faith more thoroughly, and should know how to apply all this to practical daily living. Dr. David R. Breed writes:

The first element of sermonizing is instruction. There is absolutely nothing which takes precedence of it. The preacher should be a teacher before all things else. The sermon from which the hearers learn nothing is a failure. The apostles were sent forth by the Saviour to teach as well as to preach, and Jesus Himself was emphatically a teacher. He was so regarded by His contemporaries and has been so regarded ever since. All the great leaders of religious thought from the beginning have excelled in the teaching function, and it is highly important that the teaching faculty should be developed by every one who attempts to proclaim the gospel.[9]

Teaching prepares the way for practicing, for hearers cannot be right and do right until they know what is right. This is the didactic appeal.

2. Then there is the need for *inspiration*, to set on fire the knowledge people have, to stir up lagging spirits, to infuse new courage and faith into fainting hearts. Inspiration is basic to enlistment.

3 Again, the aim may be *devotion*. The purpose is to bring the people into a worshipful sense of God's nearness and into a larger surrender to Him. This

9 David R. Breed, *Preparing to Preach*, p. 189.

objective is usually back of the prayer-meeting talk, and often motivates the Sunday morning message.

4 Another aim is that of *correction*. There come times when the Biblical duties of reproof, correction and instruction in righteousness (2 Tim. 3:16–17) are necessary. This aim is akin to that of instruction, and is based on instruction, but it is intended to provide opportunity for the Holy Spirit to effect a specific change in wrong attitudes and conduct.

5 The *conversion* aim is one constantly in the minds of evangelical preachers. The Sunday night service is usually evangelistic, and often that is the dominant note in the Sunday morning service. Every pastor should do the work of an evangelist, but, in addition, many conservative churches hold an extra evangelistic series for a week or two each year.

In evangelistic sermons one purpose is dominant —that of bringing the unsaved to an immediate public commitment to Jesus Christ as Lord and Saviour—while other aims may be to bring backsliders to a rededication to Christ, to inspire Christians to undertake personal soul-winning, to increase the number of tithers and family altars, and to cause young people to dedicate their lives to full-time Christian service.

Especially applicable to evangelistic preaching are the seven basic appeals pointed out by Dr. Charles W. Koller, president of Northern Baptist Theological Seminary, Chicago. These seven appeals to the heart Dr. Koller gives as follows:

1. *The appeal to altruism,* the spirit of benevolence or devotion to the interests of others. This appeal,

so often neglected, is always effective with certain big-souled types of men and women not reached on the basis of self-interest (Num. 10:29-33, Deut. 5:9, Luke 15:7).

2. *The appeal to aspiration,* the universal hunger for spiritual happiness, or sense of completeness. It reaches those who long for a better life (Matt. 19:20, Luke 23:42, Acts 16:14, Rev. 2:5).

3. *The appeal to curiosity,* that which appears novel, unfamiliar or mysterious. This appeal may become trashy and is subject to abuse, but has a rightful place (John 1:47, 4:10, Luke 19:5).

4. *The appeal to duty,* the divine urge to do a thing because it is right, or to refrain from a thing because it is wrong. Charles G. Finney used it often (Matt. 25:27, Acts 10:5, Jas. 3:10).

5. *The appeal to fear.* The New Testament justifies it and apparently more respond to this appeal in our times than to that of love (Jonah 3:4, Acts 9:6, 16:29, Acts 24:25).

6. *The appeal to love,* love of God, love of others, love of self. Moody used it. The supreme appeal is that to the love of Christ (Luke 10:27, 2 Cor. 5:14, 1 John 4:19).

7. *The appeal to reason,* a strong use of argument. Jonathan Edwards and Charles G. Finney used it (1 Sam. 12:7, Isa. 1:18, Acts 17:2, 17).

We must expect conversions or we will never have them. A young preacher asked Spurgeon, "Why is it that you have so many conversions, and I never seem to have any?" Spurgeon asked, "You do not expect to have conversions every time you preach, do you?" "No, certainly I don't expect anything like that," replied the young preacher. "Then that is the reason you don't have them. I aim for conversions and expect to have them every time I preach," said Spurgeon, one of the greatest evangelistic preachers of all time.

In the Yale lectures of 1876–77, Phillips Brooks said:

A sermon exists in and for its purpose. That purpose is the persuading and moving of men's souls. That purpose must never be lost sight of. If it ever is, the sermon flags.[10]

Charles G. Finney, the noted American revivalist, said:

A minister should aim to convert his congregation. But you will ask, Does not all preaching aim at this? No. A minister always has some aim in preaching, but most sermons were never aimed at converting sinners. And if sinners were converted under them, the preacher himself would be amazed.[11]

Within each of these specific aims of preaching there may be several particular ones. Under instruction, we may aim at teaching certain doctrines, or at instructing a certain class of hearers. In connection with the aim of inspiration, we may wish to enlist the audience in a program of evangelistic visitation or tithing. The devotional aim may be directed toward securing com-

10 Phillips Brooks, *Lectures on Preaching* (E. P. Dutton & Company, New York, 1898), p. 110.
11 Charles G. Finney, *Lectures on Revivals of Religion* (Fleming H. Revell Company, New York, 1898), p. 203.

mitment to full-time Christian service or to maintaining daily devotions. The aim of correction would apply to specific wrongs or errors. The conversion aim might be directed toward converting children, or men, or parents, or young people, or atheists.

Preaching without an aim is bound to be vague, generalized, dull, and uninteresting. W. E. Sangster of London has written:

That dreadful vagueness which hangs over so much preaching derives in the main from the fact that it is not clearly aiming to do something. The preacher himself has no clear object in view. It is not a matter for wonder . . . that the people also find it painfully vague.[12]

We trust that the importance of the aim in sermonizing is now apparent. The preacher must preach next Sunday morning. Perhaps his first consideration will be, "What do I wish God to accomplish through this sermon?" If this question is not in the foreground of his thinking, it must be in the background, and tends to influence his selection of the Scripture passage or theme for the message. Even if a man is preaching expository sermons through books of the Bible, the aim will influence the choice of the books to be expounded. If the aim is instruction, any of the books of the Bible may be used, but if the aim is devotion, God may lead him to Psalms; if the aim is conversion, to Romans or the Gospel of John; or if the aim is inspiration, to Isaiah or Ephesians; for correction, the Holy Spirit may direct the preacher to 1 Corinthians or James.

[12] W. E. Sangster, *The Craft of Sermon Construction* (The Westminster Press, Philadelphia, 1950), p. 137.

The authors do not claim that the aim always comes first chronologically in the preacher's thinking, though we believe it generally should. A Scripture passage or a subject may force itself on the preacher for discussion, then he may look into it for its homiletical possibilities before he formulates his aim. The aim should come near the beginning of the sermonizing process.

The primary test of any sermon is its effect upon the man in the pew. Therefore, the preacher must deliberately aim to make something happen to his hearers.

REFERENCES

Homiletics

Blocker, Simon, *The Secret of Pulpit Power Through Thematic Christian Preaching*, Grand Rapids, Michigan: W. B. Eerdmans Publishing Company, 1951, Chapter 1.

Brastow, Lewis G., *The Work of The Preacher*, Boston: The Pilgrim Press, 1914, Section 1, Chapters 1–2.

Byington, E. H., *Pulpit Mirrors*, New York: George H. Donan Co., 1927, prelude.

Jordan, G. Ray, *You Can Preach*, New York: Fleming H. Revell Company, 1951, Chapter 7.

Kidder, Daniel P., *A Treatise on Homiletics*, New York: Carlton and Lanahan, 1866, Chapter 20.

Kirkpatrick, Robert White, *The Creative Delivery of Sermons*, New York: The Macmillan Company, 1944, Chapters 3–4.

Morgan, G. Campbell, *Preaching*, New York: Fleming H. Revell Company, 1937, Chapter 1.

Shedd, William G. T., *Homiletics, and Pastoral Theology,* New York: Scribner, Armstrong and Company, 1873, Chapter 10.

Whitesell, Faris Daniel, *The Art of Biblical Preaching,* Grand Rapids: Zondervan Publishing Company, 1950, Chapter 7.

Speech

Crocker, Lionel, *Public Speaking for College Students,* Chicago: American Book Company, 1941, Chapter 16.

Dixon, John, *How To Speak,* New York: Abingdon-Cokesbury Press, 1949, Chapter 1.

Monroe, Alan Houston, *Principles and Types of Speech,* New York: Scott-Foresman and Company, 1939, Chapter 8.

Oliver, Robert Tarbell, Cortwright, R. L., and Hager, C. F., *The New Training for Effective Speech,* New York: Dryden Press, 1946, Chapter 12.

Sarett, Lew and Foster, William Trufant, *Basic Principles of Speech,* Chicago: Houghton Mifflin Company, 1936, Chapter 2.

II

Vary the Biblical Content of Your Sermons

The Bible is the unique source and fountainhead of Christian preaching, and every sermon should have Biblical support. The preacher is often tempted to minimize Biblical content in preaching in order to emphasize current events, patriotic subjects, denominational issues or psychological problems, but this can never be done without loss. He loses the inspiration of truth, the full co-operation of the Holy Spirit, and the sympathy of spiritual-minded listeners. However, such subjects as mentioned above may be discussed with Biblical support if the preacher is at home with the Bible, and is determined to be a Biblical preacher above all other things.

Since the Bible is God's unique communication of Himself and His truth to men, and is the highest and holiest source of truth, light and power, there is no reason for preachers to depart from Bible preaching. The purpose of ordination is to set men apart to preach the Word of God, and Christian pulpits are speaking places dedicated to the preaching of the Bible. The preacher is God's prophet declaring God's message to men rather than a priest officiating at an altar on men's behalf. When people come to church they expect to hear the Bible interpreted and applied to life. All the gains come to the Biblical preacher.

In 1910 Dr. Harry Jeffs of England wrote:

The world never needed Bible preaching more than it does today; people never welcomed Bible preaching from the preacher with convictions more eagerly and hungrily, and the man who can satisfy that deep hunger of the soul for Bible preaching, though he may be no dazzling genius, will find pulpits open to him wherever he goes. His bread will never fail, for the people will always provide daily bread for the man who knows how to break and distribute to them the Bread of Life.[1]

Biblical preaching[2] then is preaching with sound Biblical support, molded throughout by the teachings and spirit of the Bible. No other preaching is worth the time and effort of God's spokesmen. Lewis O. Brastow of Yale wrote:

As preaching strays away from a Biblical basis, it tends to subjectivity. It may become rationalistically subjective or mystically subjective or æsthetically subjective, according to the preacher's prevailing tendency or tendency of the time, or of the circle to which he belongs. The restoration of the Biblical quality involves a restoration of objective quality both in substance and form.[3]

The Bible itself is a book of varied literary forms, and tends to yield variety in the presentation of divine

---

[1] H. Jeffs, *The Art of Exposition* (The Pilgrim Press, Boston, 1910), p. 18.

[2] For a full discussion of Biblical preaching, see *The Art of Biblical Preaching* by F. D. Whitesell (Zondervan, Grand Rapids, 1950), 160 pages.

[3] Lewis O. Brastow, *The Work of the Preacher* (The Pilgrim Press, Boston, 1914), p. 167.

truth. It is a divine library of sixty-six varied volumes containing law, history, poetry, prophecy, wisdom literature, narratives, allegories, parables, apocalypses, biographies, chronicles, dramas, riddles, visions, sermons, songs, conversations, letters, teachings; the words of God the Father, God the Son, and God the Holy Spirit, of men, angels, archangels, demons and Satan. Such a book as the Bible could come to us only in the way it claims to have come—by divine inspiration as holy men of God spoke and wrote, moved by the Holy Spirit.

To preach the Bible in all its varying literary forms, historical phases, and doctrinal aspects is the greatest challenge that could come to any living man. How wonderful to be able to think God's thoughts after Him and with Him and to present them to needy listeners!

Three score and ten years is not time enough to allow the Biblical preacher to exhaust the depths of the Bible. The more a man preaches the Bible, the more he will wish to preach it. The deeper he goes into it, and the longer he stays with it, the more he will see in it to preach.

When Sir Frances Drake stood on the Isthmus of Panama and got his first glimpse of the mighty Pacific Ocean, he prayed, "Almighty God, of thy goodness give me life and leave to sail once in an English ship upon that Sea." The preacher should pray to be permitted to sail all his lifetime on the boundless ocean of God's Word.

Why should men waste their time, energy and

opportunities on other preaching material when the Bible gives all they need and more, and guarantees them that this preaching, if adapted to the people's needs, will do the most good to the most people over the longest period of time?

Therefore, we should consider how we can vary the Biblical content of sermons in order to get the widest possible diversity and yet remain true to the Bible, to Christ and to our ordination commission.

Homiletical authorities have classified sermons according to contents, purposes, structure, occasion, style, modes of delivery, thematic emphasis, logic of approach, and the amount of material in the text, but perhaps the most frequent classification is based on the method of handling the text—topical, textual, and expository. But in actual practice sermons do not usually fit these categories exactly. They tend to overlap and take on the character of more than one of these classifications. But since this last classification is so familiar, we will follow it, seeking to classify under each category the varying Biblical bases for sermons. Let us consider these types in the following order: expository, textual, topical.

THE EXPOSITORY METHOD

Most homileticians and preachers will award first place to this type of preaching as the most desirable, since it adheres more closely to the apostolic pattern, honors the Word more, and establishes people more firmly in the knowledge of the Word.

Definitions of expository preaching vary, but most

of them indicate that its chief emphasis is explanation of Bible passages and application of the truth. Expository preaching seeks to find the basic, contextual-grammatical-historical meaning of a passage of Scripture, and then applies this meaning, by accepted rhetorical processes, to the hearts and lives of the hearers. Expository preaching finds more than a theme in a passage, more than a few suggestions, more than a few platitudes —it finds the abiding message, the timeless truths, the universal values of the passage, and brings them over in direct, powerful, impinging practical applications to modern life situations.

Some authorities distinguish expository from textual preaching only by the length of the passage treated, but we prefer to differentiate these two by the method of handling the passage. We commend the definition of expository preaching given by John Hall in 1875:

By expository preaching we mean that in which a minister, having, by the aid of grammar, dictionary, and all proper helps, learned for himself what meaning the Holy Ghost intended to convey in the passage he has in hand, and then what uses he ought, in harmony with the rest of divine teaching, to make of it, and having filled his own understanding, and warmed his own heart with this truth, tells it to his people, with clearness, simplicity, force and fervor.[4]

Another pertinent quotation concerning the nature of expository preaching we take from the eminent expositor, W. H. Griffith Thomas:

4 John Hall, *God's Word Through Preaching*, p. 71.

If inquiry be made, it will be found that there have been very few really expository preachers in the Christian Church; expository, that is, as distinct from Biblical preachers. Spurgeon was a Biblical preacher, so was Moody, but neither of them could be called an expository preacher. Maclaren is the nearest approach to a preacher who is at once Biblical and expository, and his expositions will be found to be the finest models of all expository preaching.

Three requirements should be emphasized in every endeavor to present to our people an exposition of any passage. (1) It should concern only the *salient* features. There are many details that must be resolutely omitted, lest we are too long, and lest we blur the definite impression. (2) It should mainly concern the *spiritual* meaning. Anything historical, or geographical, or oriental, must be kept resolutely subordinated to the supreme issue; it is a sermon, not a lecture. (3) It should always have a *searching* message. The application in an exposition should be emphasized and never omitted. If these three essentials are observed; only salient; mainly spiritual; always searching; there is no reason why many of us should not develop into capable and acceptable expository preachers.[5]

We believe that every preacher should major on expository preaching. It should not be his only method, but should have an important place. Now, how can we achieve variety within this method of preaching? There are several ways.

Exposition of single verses. Some would call this textual preaching, but we prefer to classify it as expository preaching, since it follows the expository

5 W. H. Griffith Thomas, *The Work of the Ministry* (Hodder and Stoughton, New York, n.d.), pp. 229-230.

method. The outline does not necessarily depend on the parts of the text, but on its meaning and application. The exposition of the text reaches out into the context and utilizes all grammatical and historical material. But in true textual preaching the theme comes from the text, and the main points come from the main divisions of the text, with no attention necessarily given to context, grammar or historical background. Dr. Thomas made the following comment about Maclaren:

Dr. Maclaren's textual preaching is essentially expository, even though it deals with one verse only, because it is thoroughly Biblical and arises immediately out of the text.[6]

Exposition of paragraphs. The paragraphing of the American Standard Version or the Revised Standard Version usually gives an ideal unit for expository preaching. Since a paragraph is a complete thought progression containing several verses, it is not difficult to find a theme and full supporting material within a Scripture paragraph. One such unit, properly selected, will give the preacher all the material he can well manage in a single sermon.

In this method of preaching, the theme, the proposition, the main divisions, and the major supporting thoughts come directly from the paragraph and its context. The whole development stays with the passage and its context in the most conscientious effort to teach exactly what God meant that passage to teach.

There are literally hundreds of suitable paragraphs for expository work scattered throughout the Bible.

[6] W. H. Griffith Thomas, *idem.,* p. 229.

Some men find it profitable to expound books of the Bible in sermon courses, or series, one sermon to a paragraph, until they have covered the whole book. This method can be used with the small books of the Bible, but for the larger books, like those of the Pentateuch, the four Gospels, Acts, Romans, or the Revelation, such a procedure might become too tedious. Some of the church fathers and Puritan preachers spent two or three years preaching through a book of the Bible, but that would not be welcomed today by an American congregation. Such an undertaking would militate against the very thing we are advocating—variety in preaching.

But to preach through the large books of the Bible, the expository preacher would have either to take more than one paragraph at a time, or else select the outstanding paragraphs and let the others go; or use whole chapters; or follow thematic divisions of the book in sections longer than chapters. To discover properly divided sections, consult Bible study outlines in books of Biblical introduction. Whatever size portions of Scripture the expository preacher uses, the same methods would apply, except that with the very long passages he could not pay as much attention to details.

When it comes to obtaining the structure for the expository sermon, one may take the leading ideas as they emerge from his exegetical study; or he may take a key verse in the passage and let its ideas reach out and include the whole section; or he may find certain important words, ideas, or well-known verses recurring in the passage which can form an outline; or, in a narrative

section, he may tell the story graphically and chronologically, and draw out the lessons afterwards; or sometimes he may force a breakdown of the section by
asking what the passage teaches about God or human
responsibility.

Some expositors ignore structure by following a
verse-by-verse commenting method, emphasizing the
important thoughts in each verse, Dr. Byington of
Gordon College, Boston, used to call this "the string-of-
pearls" method. Men who preach acceptably without
stable homilectical structure must compensate for its
lack by able use of explanatory, illustrative and applicatory material.

Exposition of Bible chapters. There are 1189 chapters in the Bible, and many of them make good expository preaching units as they stand. Generally, Christians have their favorite chapters, and enjoy hearing
each discussed as a whole. Every preacher should make
a place now and then for sermons on Bible chapters.
But chapter preaching is often more difficult than
paragraph preaching. The two difficulties are the large
amount of material and its proper organization. Dr. A.
W. Blackwood says:

Preaching from the chapter is more difficult than anything
we have considered thus far. The increased difficulty is due
to the greater length of the passage. On the other hand, if
the chapter sermon lives up to its possibilities, it is almost
certain to be popular.[7]

Let the preacher begin with some of the easier

7 A. W. Blackwood, *Preaching from the Bible* (Abingdon-Cokesbury
Press, New York, 1941), p. 135.

chapters, those having unity, action, vividness, and not too long, such as Psalm 1 and Mark 5. Some of the favorite chapters of Christians, like John 14 and Romans 8, are not necessarily the easiest ones to handle. The sermonizer should try the less difficult chapters first, until he has gained experience and confidence before he asks the people to request sermons on their favorite chapters.

When the preacher studies a Bible chapter as a whole, in the light of its setting, and with the aid of his commentaries, he will find a theme and a structure for a message. In making a plan, it is well to avoid clever, artificial and strained outlines and hold to the more practical and self-evident divisions. The outline is important and should not strike the people as something foreign to the thought and context of the chapter, or as something forced on it. Main divisions should be natural, clear, individualistic, interesting, progressive and symmetrical.

Exposition of thematic sections. The section or division may be longer than a chapter; in fact, it may contain several chapters. In some cases it may be shorter than a chapter, but it constitutes a logical discussion of one main theme of a Bible book. Many Bible books have an introduction and a conclusion shorter than a chapter, but which stand as separate units in the thought of the book, and deserve separate discussion.

In a book like Romans, if one were preaching through it by sections, he would perhaps preach on the introduction, 1:1–7, first; or he might enlarge the introduction to include the theme of the book, 1:1–17.

If he took the longer passage for his opening message, he would probably take as his next passage the long section, 1:18—3:20, which constitutes one thematic unit, showing the reasons for the wrath of God on both Gentile and Jew. His third message might deal with God's remedy for man's condemnation, centering in justification, and his section would be Romans 3:21—4:25.

In these long sections the synthetic method, by which we combine the component parts into one whole, is necessary. We need to use the analytic method, by which we break up the whole into its component parts, to discover what is in the passage, but the synthetic method to put it together into a unity for preaching.

Exposition of whole Bible books. Here the idea is to preach one sermon on a whole book of the Bible, seeking to bring out its main teachings in an interesting, practical and helpful way. This is about the longest section the preacher should take for expository preaching although we heard of one man who claimed that he preached an expository sermon on the whole Bible!

Since the books of the Bible vary in length from one chapter in Philemon and Jude to 150 chapters in the Psalms, and since there is much more unity in a book like Genesis than in a book like Proverbs, we can see that it is difficult to apply one method to all the books of the Bible. But we do hold that the expository method is the best one for handling the books of the Bible either singly or in a sermonic series.

We will wish to understand each Bible book in the light of its chronology, times, authorship, contents,

and setting in the unfolding of progressive divine revelation. We will seek its one theme, and its timeless
truths, or abiding lessons, and bring them to bear on
life today. We suggest that in preparation for such
a sermon the preacher read his chosen Bible book
through several times with pencil in hand, that he
read the appropriate chapter in G. Campbell Morgan's
The Messages of the Books of the Bible and in H. H.
Halley's *Pocket Bible Handbook* and that he read what
some of the books of Bible introduction have to say
about that particular Bible book. We recommend Merrill F. Unger's *Old Testament Introduction* and Henry
C. Thiessen's *New Testament Introduction,* and the
articles in the conservative Bible dictionaries and encyclopedias.

Like chapter preaching, so in preaching expository
sermons on the books of the Bible, it is well to take
first the shorter books like Ruth and Jonah, having
unity, color and movement, then to pass on to the more
complex and doctrinal books like Leviticus and Hebrews. In such preaching there is great power and
profit for both preacher and people.

We have given first place in significance and value
to the expository method of handling the Scriptures—
the contextual-grammatical-historical approach, and
have suggested various length passages to which it can
be applied.

We should recognize that in expository preaching
the exposition will be close, analytical and microscopic
if the passage is short; but loose, synthetic and tele-
scopic as the passage lengthens. But either way, if the

main efforts are to explain and apply the primary contextual-grammatical-historical teachings of the passage
with a searching spiritual emphasis, the method is expository.

THE TEXTUAL METHOD

Here the text is usually a single verse of Scripture,
occasionally two or three verses. The purpose is to get
a theme from the text, then to derive the main points
from the main parts of the text. The development may
stay close to the text or it may go far and wide for
supporting materials.

The textual method gives more liberty to bring
in extra-Biblical ideas and supporting material than
does the expository method. Not so much concerned
with context, grammar, and backgrounds as the expository sermon, it gives more room for the injection of
personal ideas and concepts.

Some authorities would call the sermon textual
even if the expository method of handling the text
were used. Dr. Blackwood distinguishes the textual
from the expository by the length of the passage used
rather than by our distinction based on the method of
treating the passages. Whatever the label we use, we
can easily see that the Bible offers a great variety of
attractive texts.

We find evangelistic texts, inspirational texts,
comforting texts, devotional texts, doctrinal texts, re-
buking texts, ethical texts, historical texts. Some texts
are in the form of statements, while others are in the
form of questions; some are commands, some exhorta-

tions and some exclamations. Some are prose, some are poetry; some literal and some figurative. There are key texts which unlock a book, as 1 John 5:13, "These things have I written unto you that believe on the name of the Son of God: that ye may know that ye have eternal life, and that ye may believe on the name of the Son of God"; and others are incidental texts, as 1 Thessalonians 5:26, "Greet all the brethren with an holy kiss." There are integrated texts, as 1 Corinthians 13:7, "Beareth all things, believeth all things, hopeth all things, endureth all things"; and isolated texts, as Matthew 7:6, "Give not that which is holy unto the dogs, neither cast ye your pearls before swine, lest they trample them under their feet, and turn again and rend you."

There are familiar texts, as John 3:16, "For God so loved the world, that he gave his only begotten Son, that whosoever believeth in him should not perish, but have everlasting life," and unfamiliar texts, as Jude 11 "Woe unto them! for they have gone in the way of Cain, and ran greedily after the error of Balaam for reward, and perished in the gainsaying of Core."

Many books of the Bible have one text that is the theme of the book, as discussed in A. T. Pierson's book, *Key Words of the Bible*. Most chapters of the Bible have a key-verse text at their heart. See G. Campbell Morgan's *Searchlights of the Word* for a sermonette on one text out of each chapter of the Bible. Austin Phelps says that the great texts are dense points of divine revelation and that we cannot afford to ignore them. They demand that we preach on them if we are Biblical preachers. The expository preacher, as he deals with large portions of the Word, will uncover many single texts which he will wish to treat separately on other occasions.

THE TOPICAL METHOD

Our third method of varying the Biblical basis of preaching is the topical. Here the theme is derived from the text but treated separately from it with the support of other passages; or else the theme is chosen apart from any one text, but a number of Bible passages are used to support the main points of the message. Biblical themes can be treated as found in the whole Bible, or as discussed in the writings of individual Bible authors, or as developed in a single book or chapter of the Bible.

Dr. Blackwood claims that practically all the famous sermons of Christian history have been topical sermons. Perhaps the reason for this is that the topical method allows the preacher unlimited opportunity to concentrate on a single theme. He is not bound by a single text, large or small. He can develop the theme logically, chronologically, historically, geographically, or psychologically with all the force and fervor at his command.

Such books as *The New Topical Textbook,* Nave's *Topical Bible,* Hitchcock's *Topical Analysis,* or Cruden's *Concordance* will suggest almost an unlimited supply of subjects and themes for topical preaching. See Chapter III for examples of Biblical subjects and themes drawn from a single subject.

On the whole, the topical method is the easiest type of preaching and therein its dangers lie. It is relatively easy to find a theme and to compile a number of verses bearing on it, and then discuss these verses under the separate points of the sermon. No thorough contextual-grammatical-historical exegesis is required.

The Bible reading is a rather rambling form of topical discussion which uses a large number of scattered passages. This approach always tempts to loose structure.[8]

The danger with the topical method is that usually it does not require the hard exegetical, analytical, logical study that the expository and textual methods require. It tends to lift texts out of their context and does not teach the Bible against the background of its history and chronology.

Some preachers continually fall back on their topical textbooks or the topical studies in Thompson's *Chain Reference Bible* for their sermon themes. They rest on the results of some other person's topical work rather than going beyond them to complete preparation. Thus their sermons lack vitality and originality. But if a man will work out a theme thoroughly, using his concordances, lexicons, theology books, and all other aids, he will be able to produce interesting and helpful topical messages. This method has a place in the scheme of preaching, and certain occasions may demand it, but it should not have a primary place, in the opinion of the authors.

[8] For a fuller treatment of Bible reading, see F. D. Whitesell, *The Art of Biblical Preaching*, pp. 39–44.

REFERENCES

Homiletics

Broadus, John A., *On The Preparation and Delivery of Sermons,* New York: Harper & Brothers, 1944, Part II, Chapter 5.

Etter, J. W., *The Preacher and His Sermon,* Dayton, Ohio: United Brethren Publishing House, 1891, Part II, Chapter 7.

Knott, Harold E., *How To Prepare an Expository Sermon,* Cincinnati: The Standard Publishing Company, 1930.

Meyer, F. B., *Expository Preaching Plans and Methods,* New York: George H. Doran Company, 1912.

Montgomery, R. Ames, *Expository Preaching,* New York: Fleming H. Revell Company, 1939.

Ray, Jeff D., *Expository Preaching,* Grand Rapids, Michigan: Zondervan Publishing House, 1940.

Whitesell, F. D., *The Art of Biblical Preaching,* Grand Rapids: Zondervan Publishing Company, 1950, Chapter 2.

III

Vary the Subjects, Themes and Titles of Your Sermons

Of utmost importance in preaching is the process of selecting sermon subjects, drawing out good themes, and phrasing attractive titles. The Holy Spirit's aid here should be sought especially. One of the most frequent criticisms of expository preaching has been that it was so often separated from the needs of the people. This fault can be overcome, in large measure, by proper attention to subjects, themes and titles. These terms are not synonymous.

The *subject* tells what the sermon is about. The *theme* indicates that particular aspect of the subject which will be most useful for presentation to the people. The *title* gives the final phrasing of the theme as it goes into the bulletin, the newspaper, and on the bulletin board. It covers the same idea as the theme but may be worded quite differently to make it interesting and attractive. We prefer not to use the word, "topic," because it is often used identically with the words, "theme," "title," "subject."

The *subject,* then, is the general or class idea.[1] It

[1] John F. Genung, *Working Principles of Rhetoric,* 1900, p. 249.

represents the broad area out of which a number of specific themes may be chosen, and normally is expressed in one word. Subjects tend to be limited in number because of their breadth. In 1891, Thomas J. Potter wrote:

It is very important to make a good selection of the subject on which we intend to preach. The subject is the foundation of our discourse, and unless the materials of the foundation be directly chosen and well adapted to their purpose the edifice will scarcely be either sound or pleasing.[2]

We can best show the broad general nature of subjects by listing below a number taken from the Bible:

1. Affliction	17. Fellowship
2. Angels	18. Forgiveness
3. Atonement	19. Grace
4. Baptism	20. Heaven
5. Brotherhood	21. Hell
6. Christ	22. Holiness
7. The Church	23. The Holy Spirit
8. Compromise	24. Honor
9. Conscience	25. Hope
10. Courage	26. Humility
11. The Cross	27. Idolatry
12. Death	28. Judgment
13. Discipleship	29. Justification
14. Divorce	30. Law
15. Faith	31. Love
16. Fear	32. Missions

2 Thomas J. Potter, *Sacred Eloquence* (Fr. Pustet & Company, New York and Cincinnati, 1891), p. 69.

33. Obedience	42. Self-control
34. Patience	43. Sin
35. Peace	44. Stewardship
36. Praise	45. Thanksgiving
37. Prayer	46. Unity
38. Redemption	47. Witnessing
39. Resurrection	48. Work
40. Sacrifice	49. Worry
41. The Second Coming	50. Worship

We might possibly exhaust the subjects in the Bible, but it would hardly be possible to exhaust the themes in the Bible. David R. Breed points this out in the following incident:

A young minister once remarked to an older one, "I fear that I shall not be able to continue in the pulpit. . . ." "Why so?" "Because I have exhausted all of my material. I have preached upon *all the subjects* I can think of. . . ." "Suppose, then," said the elder, "you now begin to preach upon texts." The young man perceived his mistake and was led to apprehend the proper method to his immediate relief and his subsequent manifest growth.[3]

When the general subject is specifically defined, the resulting phrase, normally, of three or more words will be the *theme* of the message. The theme is that particular approach to the subject which will be more easily grasped by the people and more easily developed by the preacher. As a ray of light may be broken into the various colors of the spectrum by passing it through a prism, so a subject may be broken up into a large

[3] David R. Breed, *Preparing to Preach*, p. 50.

number of themes by passing it through the mind's analytical processes.

Subjects are broad and difficult to handle, as they stand, but themes are specific aspects of a subject, and, consequently, much easier to discuss. We need to distinguish these concepts sharply. In 1905, Dr. Arthur S. Hoyt showed how this difficulty had plagued preachers through the years when he said:

> The words "subject" and "theme" are used by many interchangeably, but it is a loose use of terms, the result of hazy thought and indefinite aim. The subject is general; the theme is particular. "Faith" is a subject; "The Promptitude of Faith" is a theme. "Faith" is broad and general; it makes no affirmation or denial; it suggests no limit or purpose. "The Promptitude of Faith" is specific, gives definite relations and has an unmistakable purpose.[4]

This failure to limit the subject before attempting to prepare a message also has been noted in the field of secular public speaking by Oliver, Cortright and Hager in the following quotation:

> Probably the most frequent error of the beginner consists in selecting topics that are too broad. Here are a few subjects upon which some students have vainly struggled. . . . "The Causes, Kinds, and Cures for Insanity," "Policy," "The New Deal," "The World in 1975."[5]

The theme should be plain, clear, brief and comprehensive of the substance of the sermon. It divides

4 Arthur S. Hoyt, *The Work of Preaching* (George H. Doran & Company, New York, 1905), p. 98.
5 Oliver, Cortright, and Hager, *The New Training for Effective Speech* (The Dryden Press, New York, 1946), p. 155.

the subject, or suggests relationships, or infers an affirmation about the subject. The theme brings definiteness of aim and unity of thought. Genung says: "The theme is the subject turned into a certain determinate direction."[6] The process of limiting a subject through the use of themes will be seen as we take the subject of "Prayer" and list some of the possible themes that can be drawn from it.

1. The necessity of prayer
2. The value of prayer
3. The times for prayer
4. The power of prayer
5. The purpose of prayer
6. The methods of prayer
7. The results of prayer
8. The conditions of prayer
9. The problems of prayer
10. Praying in the Spirit
11. Perseverance in prayer
12. The pre-eminence of prayer
13. Answers to prayer
14. Intercessory prayer
15. Family prayer
16. Hindrances to prayer
17. Bible prayers
18. Practical prayer
19. Attitudes in prayer
20. Places to pray
21. Worship through prayer
22. Posture in prayer
23. The privilege of prayer
24. Faith and prayer
25. The scope of prayer

The more specific the theme, so long as it is important, the more suggestive it will be, and the easier it will be to handle. The example given above demon-

[6] John F. Genung, *op. cit.*, p. 421.

strates the fact that the number of themes on Biblical subjects is virtually inexhaustible.

The *title* for a sermon is the announced or advertised form of the theme: the thought is the same but the title is phrased for bulletin board appeal. The theme, "The Necessity of Prayer," might be advertised under the title of "You Must Pray," or, "The Inevitability of Prayer." Dr. Arthur J. Gossip uses the title, "The Day-Dreams of a Christian Man," for his sermon on Philippians 3:10, "That I may know him and the power of his resurrection . . .," in which he discusses the theme (though not formally expressed), "Knowing Christ."

Frederick W. Robertson preached on Hebrews 11:8–10:

By faith Abraham, when he was called to go out into a place which he should after receive for an inheritance, obeyed; and he went out, not knowing whither he went. By faith he sojourned in the land of promise, as in a strange country, dwelling in tabernacles with Isaac and Jacob, the heirs with him of the same promise; for he looked for a city which hath foundations, whose builder and maker is God.

He developed the thought that Abraham never received the land of Canaan during his lifetime as a possession; he looked beyond for something better. His theme drawn from this passage was, "Unfulfilled Promises," but his title was, "The Illusiveness of Life."

J. H. Jowett took the text, "Sleeping for Sorrow," Luke 22:45, and found in it the theme, "Alleviating Sorrow," but he preached his sermon under the title,

"Divine Amelioratives." Dr. James W. Brougher, Sr., was preaching in Los Angeles on Genesis 3, the fall in the Garden of Eden. His theme was, "Hiding from God," but his title was, "The First Runaway Couple."

Sarett and Foster,[7] from the viewpoint of secular public speaking, say that a title should suggest but not explicitly state the main idea of the speech; it should be in keeping with the mood of the speech, the character of the audience and the nature of the occasion; it should be as concrete as possible; and it should arouse curiosity. George M. Glasgow[8] says that a title should create interest, be brief, condensed, compact and energetic, and should reveal the nature of the subject. Dr. Andrew W. Blackwood[9] warns against sameness, tameness and lameness of titles and advises to make them interesting but not sensational, clear but not revelatory, short but not abrupt, rhythmical but not to the extreme, accurate but not pedantic, and religious but not otherworldly.

Sometimes the theme and title may be identical. The phraseology of the theme may be perfectly suitable for a title. Dr. George L. Robinson preached on 1 Timothy 3:16, using the words, "The Mystery of Godliness," for both the theme and the title.

While it is perhaps true that very few additional hearers are attracted to church by advertised sermon titles, yet those who attend habitually are interested in

---

[7] Sarett and Foster, *Basic Principles of Speech*, revised (Houghton, Mifflin Company, 1946), pp. 325–328.

[8] Geo. M. Glasgow, *Dynamic Public Speaking*, p. 64.

[9] Andrew W. Blackwood, *The Preparation of Sermons* (Abingdon-Cokesbury, New York, 1948). pp. 91–95.

them. A well-phrased title tends to stimulate both the audience and the preacher. A wise selection of subjects, a varied range of themes, and careful sermon titling promotes that variety which we seek.

REFERENCES

Homiletics

Blackwood, Andrew Watterson, *The Preparation of Sermons*, Nashville: Abingdon-Cokesbury Press, 1948, Chapter 8.

Blocker, Simon, *The Secret of Pulpit Power through Thematic Christian Preaching*, Grand Rapids, Michigan: W. B. Eerdmans Publishing Company, 1951, Chapter 2.

Brastow, Lewis O., *The Work of the Preacher*, Boston: The Pilgrim Press, 1914, Chapter 2.

Broadus, John A., *On the Preparation and Delivery of Sermons*, New York: Harper Brothers, 1944, Part I, Chapter 3.

Pattison, T. Harwood, *The Making of the Sermon*, Philadelphia: The American Baptist Publication Society, 1898, Chapters 7, 8, 9.

Reu, M., *Homiletics, A Manual of the Theory and Practice of Preaching*, Minneapolis: Augsburg Publishing House, 1950, Chapter 16.

Speech

Hayworth, Donald, *Introduction to Public Speaking*, New York: Ronald Press, 1941, Chapter 3.

Oliver, Robert Tarbell, Cortwright, R. L., and Hager, C. F., *The New Training for Effective Speech*, New York: Dryden Press, 1946, Chapter 7.

IV

Vary the Homiletical Creativity Essential to Your Sermons

One of the heaviest responsibilities resting on the preacher is that of rightly interpreting the Word of God to his people. Many of them will know only the amount and range of truth that he gives them, and they will form their ideas of the Bible from the way he interprets it.

In this chapter we seek to show the factors involved in productive sermonic Bible study. This study will enable the preacher to come into direct contact with the infinite variety inherent in the Scriptures, which variety will stimulate homiletical creativity in the preacher. We shall discuss the man, the motives, and the methods.

THE MAN

The Bible is different from other books in that we must be in sympathy with it, and be guided by the same Spirit who inspired it if we are to fathom its spiritual riches. The better the preacher knows the author, the better he can appreciate His Word.

1. The preacher must be regenerated and Spirit-filled. Conversion, or the new birth, must be a reality to him, and he must have the spiritual outlook on life, 1 Corinthians 2:14, "But the natural man receiveth not the things of the Spirit of God: for they are foolishness unto him; neither can he know them, because they are spiritually discerned."

2. He should have confidence in the Bible as the fully inspired Word of God able to provide him with abundant preaching material. In addition to this, he should have a thorough knowledge of the Bible, so that from his storehouse of Biblical knowledge he can quickly formulate themes from Bible texts. This knowledge will equip him with a grasp of the great fundamental doctrines of the Bible and he will interpret all passages in harmony with them.

3. The preacher must be a prayerful man, depending on the Holy Spirit for that over-and-above illumination and help which books cannot give him. He should believe that his greatest assistance comes from the Spirit as he prays over his text and seeks power to impress it on the minds and consciences of his people.

THE MOTIVES

The purpose must be correct interpretation. A few presuppositions underlie the process of sound interpretation, and they will have a determinative influence on the interpreter.

1. There is only one basic, contextual-grammatical-historical meaning to any passage of Scripture. There may be several traditional interpretations, or

inferred meanings, but none of them may contain the full extent of the true meaning.

2. The preacher's responsibility is to ascertain that one true interpretation and to abide by it. This he must do even though some other interpretation may seem more scholarly or offer more preaching possibilities. Dr. David Breed writes:

Having found the meaning of this text, he must abide by it, whatever befall. He may not seek to modify it in any way; he may not attempt to relax the conditions which it imposes upon the faith or life of those to whom his sermon is addressed. He must not seek to neutralize this special text by something which he imports into it from his understanding of some other text of Scripture.[1]

3. Finally, the interpreter must be willing not only to ascertain the true meaning, to abide by it, but also to live by it. This meaning must come with power to his own heart and life before he can preach it effectively to others. Only that which comes from the heart will go to the heart. Truth must be obeyed, or practiced, before it can be transmitted vitally to others. Dr. M. Reu says:

The preacher will ask himself what message the text has for his own life; what it contains for him of reproof, comfort or incentive; . . . This is the surest way of finding what elements in the text will most appèal to and influence his hearers.[2]

[1] David R. Breed, *Preparing to Preach* (Hodder and Stoughton, New York, 1911), p. 34.
[2] M. Reu, *Homiletics* (Augsburg Publishing House, Minneapolis, 1950), pp. 382–383.

THE METHODS

1. The method of selecting the passage for your sermon text. The passage should be an appropriate one for the audience, for the occasion, for the speaker's background, and for the preacher's purpose in preaching.

The subjective moods of the preacher will be powerful in determining passages for exposition. There will be passages which impress the preacher while reading the Bible devotionally. He may see the possibility of a sermon in some verse or paragraph and feel he would like to preach on it. At other times, a passage flashes into his mind, with an outline already unfolded. Some passages with good homiletical possibilities will not be used immediately because of the restraint of the Holy Spirit.

The needs of the people will always be in the pastor's mind, and will consciously or unconsciously motivate him in selecting passages on which to preach. This thought is discussed further in Chapter XII.

The planned preaching program, as discussed in Chapter XII, will provide an abundance of good preaching passages, each of which comes up in its scheduled turn.

2. The method of analyzing the background of the passage. The first attack on the text should be to compile the factual data concerning it. Certain historical facts pertain to every book of the Bible, and contextually to every passage in the book. To ascertain these facts is to take a long stride down the road of correct interpretation. Dr. Charles W. Koller, president

of Northern Baptist Theological Seminary, Chicago, suggests seven items of factual data:

(1) *The speaker or writer:* who spoke the words of the text, God, prophet, apostle, fool, devil or saint?

(2) *The addressee:* were the words of the text written or spoken originally to believers, unbelievers, backsliders, Sanhedrin, Areopagus, a church, town people or country people?

(3) *The time:* the approximate year, and in some cases, the season of the year; and the significance of the time in relation to other contemporaneous events For this item, consult the Thompson *Chain Reference Bible* or Halley's *Pocket Bible Handbook*.

(4) *The place:* city, country, mountain, or sea; significance attached to the place; and other important events occurring in the same place.

(5) *The occasion:* the circumstances calling forth the message.

(6) *The aim:* what response was desired when it was first presented?

(7) *The theme:* what is the theme of the passage?

To these items of factual data we might add two others which will give help on some passages:

(8) *The archeological light:* has archeological research turned up any data bearing on this passage?

(9) *The writer's distinctive doctrines, ideas, and stylistic traits:* some Biblical writers approach doctrines in a different way from that of others, or they use words distinctively, *e.g.,* Paul and James on justification.

These factual data should be carefully recorded, with the Bible references for each, where available; and if any homiletical ideas emerge, they too should be recorded. The task of compiling the factual data gives the preacher an assignment to do as soon as he enters his study.

3. The method of analyzing the passage. *Make an analytical outline.* The purpose here is to find out exactly what is in the passage, and to indicate it in outline form. Dr. Koller says:

The analysis should lift out the skeleton of the passage, making the structure and progression of thought more clearly visible. It should break up the passage into paragraphic divisions, to be represented by main points; and subdivisions of paragraphs, to be represented by subheads.[3]

The idea of the analytical outline is not to make a sermon outline, but to find out the actual contents of the passage. In expository preaching on paragraphs, or longer sections, this process is very essential. There is no attempt to rearrange the ideas of the passage or to put the points in parallel structure.

In a good analytical outline the preacher records the main ideas of the passage, and the subsidiary ideas

3 Charles W. Koller, *Senior Preaching Class Notes*, 1949–50.

and their relation to the major ones. As an aid in making the analytical outline the homilist should note any change of speakers or of persons addressed; any transitional clauses or phrases; any repetition of key words or phrases; any pairing, grouping or parallelism of ideas; any contrast, opposition or interchange of ideas; any cumulative progression of ideas; any indication of cause and effect, and any division of the whole into its parts. Another aid is to check the outlines of your passage in books of Biblical introduction.

Once in a while the analytical outline can be used as a sermon outline; more often as a Sunday School lesson outline, or skeleton for a prayer-meeting message, but usually it is not structurally cohesive and is far short of being a sermon outline.

Make an analytical exegesis. John Hall in the Yale lectures of 1875, said:

For remember that the great business of your life is to be the exegesis of the Holy Word. You may not call it by that name to the people: call it opening up the Scriptures, reasoning out of them, anything you will, only provided you have the thing. To know, with the aid of grammar, dictionary, collation, and examination of argument, what the Spirit of God intended to convey in a passage, is a first requisite to honest, faithful and effective preaching. With all your gettings get the capacity to do that.[4]

Read the passage in five versions with a specific purpose in mind each time.

(1) Read the entire passage in the Williams' trans-

[4] John Hall, *God's Word Through Preaching* (Willing and Williamson, Toronto, 1875), p. 88.

lation for enjoyment sake, seeking the dominant impression. Put that dominant impression into a declarative sentence.

(2) Read the passage in the American Standard Version, noting the persons in the passage. Determine which are major and which are minor. Write your major impression about each major person.

(3) Read the passage in the original Hebrew or Greek in order to find the repeated words, phrases, and ideas, e.g., the word "straightway" in Mark 1.

(4) Read the selection at least once aloud from the King James version with the purpose of preparing to read it from the pulpit, and also to grasp any poetical significance. Poetry was written to be read aloud, not silently.

(5) Read the passage in another version of your own choosing (Revised Standard, Weymouth, Moffatt, Berkeley, Goodspeed, Phillips, or a modern foreign language version) for the purpose of finding a distinctive name for that passage, e.g., Luke 15, The Lost and Found Department of the New Testament; Hebrews 11, God's Hall of Fame.

Now make a grammatical survey of the passage. This will be microscopic in nature.

(1) Diagram the passage from the standpoint of ideas presented. This is especially helpful with important, or complex, sentences, e.g., John 1:1–18:

Analysis of Prologue of John's Gospel

The Word was in the beginning
    with God

was God
    was in the beginning with God
                    made all things
The life was in God
    was the light of men
            shined in the darkness
                apprehended it not
There (came) a man named John—(was sent)
    from God
    for a witness
    that he might bear witness
        of the light
          that all men might believe through him
   he was not the light, but came that he might bear
   witness of the light
There was the true light
       which lighteth every man coming into the world
       in the world
       the instrument in making the world
       came to *his own*
           did not receive him
And the Word became flesh, and we beheld his glory
    dwelt among us   as of the only begotten
    full of grace and truth   from the Father
John beareth witness of Him
    crieth saying—This was he of whom I said, He that
          cometh after me is become before
          me for he was before me, for of his
          fulness we all received, and grace
          for grace.

The law was given through Moses.
Grace and truth came through Jesus
Christ.

No man hath seen God at any time.
The only begotten Son hath declared him
    who is in the bosom of the Father.

(2) Take special note of the punctuation marks, e.g., the colon signifies that which precedes is equivalent to that which follows it; the question mark in Hebrews 2:4 completes the interrogation started in 2:3.

(3) Insert transitional words and phrases which help to carry a unified meaning throughout the passage, e.g., so, then, therefore, hence, on the other hand, because (Psalm 23:1, "The Lord is my shepherd, *therefore* I shall not want.")

(4) Check the meaning of all difficult words as they appear in the original Hebrew or Greek. Use a lexicon or Young's or Strong's comprehensive concordance.

(5) Check the connotation of these difficult words in the light of the time when they were written. See such word-study books as those by Girdlestone, Trench, A. T. Robertson, Wuest, and Bullinger.

(6) Check present-day synonyms and antonyms of these difficult words in Webster's Dictionary of Synonyms or Roget's Thesaurus.

(7) Note the verb tenses, especially in the Greek. The Williams and Montgomery translations are valuable at this point.

(8) Observe the word order in the original language, e.g., the emphatic words always come first in the sentence in Greek.

(9) Give attention to the figures of speech in the passage, with a view to exactness of interpretation and added color.

(10) Note repeated, peculiar, or distinctive terms as giving a clue to the writer's habits of thought.

Make a grammatical exegesis of the passage. For single texts, the grammatical custom of diagramming a sentence will prove revealing. The process shows graphically the major parts of a sentence, the modifiers of each, and their relations.

Dr. Merrill C. Tenney, in *Galatians, the Charter of Christian Liberty*, Chapter VIII, goes into considerable detail explaining how to analyze a long passage of Scripture. There is first the mechanical layout, which means rewriting the text in a form that will show its grammatical structure. The main statements are written from the extreme left-hand side of the page, and the modifiers indented, those that follow being placed below. The second part of the analysis is to create an outline from the rearranged text. This turns main statements into main points of the outline, and modifiers into sub-points. The third part of the process is observing the phenomena of the text now revealed. Says Dr. Tenney:

Such procedure is similar to preparing a dinner: mechanical analysis is like preparing the food for serving; the outline is like setting the table and arranging the courses; and the observations are like the portions which the diner selects as he fills his plate.[5]

The purpose of exegesis is to find out the true meaning of each word grammatically and in its setting in this particular passage. The two major questions that exegesis answers are: What does the passage say? and What does it mean by what it says?

In this process, the use of grammars, lexicons, word-study books, and exegetical commentaries will be necessary. The preacher should make full notes of his exegetical study and add any illustrative and applicatory ideas which come to him. Exegesis is a major part in the homiletical process of "invention." Exegesis notes tenses, moods, number, cases, and shades of meaning. It observes the various forms of speech, such as parables, parallelism, hyperbole, allegory, etc. It heeds the different types of sentence structure, noting which words and phrases are in the emphatic locations.

A good knowledge of the Hebrew and Greek is essential to the best exegetical work. Yet the man without this knowledge need not feel entirely helpless. The word-study books of such grammarians as M. Vincent, A. T. Robertson, W. E. Vine, and K. Wuest on the New Testament will help him. The exegetical commentaries will furnish help and some of the modern translations of the Bible will stand him in good stead.

Exegetical study provides the preacher with relatively original material, gives him new ideas, and often leads him into an interpretation of a passage different

[5] Merrill C. Tenney, *Galatians, the Charter of Christian Liberty* (William B. Eerdmans Publishing Company, Grand Rapids, 1950), pp. 165–173.

from the familiar ones. He should not hastily reject an interpretation because it is new to him. If he feels that it is the right one he is duty bound to hold to it. Good exegetical work discovers the infinite variety of thought and meaning inherent in the Bible and is a strong aid to variety in preaching.

Make a synthesis, or paraphrase, of the passage. The homiletical process, up to this stage, has unearthed a vast amount of material. In order to get a synthetic view of the passage as a whole, in the light of exegetical studies, it is well to paraphrase it, or make a prècis. In a paraphrase the preacher rewrites the passage in his own words, putting into it the meaning which he now believes it really conveys. Prècis writing means a "cut-down statement," one containing the essence of the material dealt with and expressed in accurate, concise form. Either process is reproduction not recreation.

The paraphrasing and prècis processes force the sermonizer to grasp the true meaning of his text, to express its central idea, to indicate the essential details, and, all in all, to clarify and fix his thinking about the passage. Speech books on oral interpretation contain helpful ideas in this regard.

4. The method of analyzing the theme. After the preacher has derived his theme from the passage of Scripture, he will need to go outside the passage in hand for more information in order to understand the theme in all of its ramifications. The process of getting this information we call analyzing the theme. We are suggesting processes of thematic analysis for three different types of themes.

(1) *Doctrinal*

(a) What is the definition of the terms of the theme:

its meaning according to the etymology of the word,

its meaning according to its usage in the Bible,

its meaning according to non-Biblical usage?

(b) What is the importance of this doctrine in the light of the whole pattern of Biblical truth?

(c) What will be results of the operation of this truth in personal experience?

(d) How is personal faith related to this doctrine?

(2) *Ethical*

(a) What is the definition of the terms of the theme:

its meaning according to the etymology of the word,

its exemplification in Biblical and non-Biblical areas,

its meaning according to negation—what it is not,

its meaning in the light of quotations from great writers,

its meaning in the light of its synonyms and antonyms?

(b) When this ethical principle prevails,

what relationship does it establish between
the individual and God, and between the
individual and his fellow men?

(c) How can this ethical principle be realized
in the individual's experience?

(d) What is its relationship to other ethical
principles? (cf. Gal. 5:22–23.)

(3) *Biographical*

(a) What is the meaning of the individual's
name?

(b) What is the ancestral background?

(c) What significant religious and secular
crises occurred in this life?

(d) What advantages for personal development were enjoyed?

(e) What traits of character were manifested?

(f) What important friendships did this person have?

(g) What important influences did this individual exert?

(h) What failures and faults occurred in this
life?

(i) What important contributions were made?

(j) What one main lesson is in this life for you?

5. The method of applying the text. Once the
meaning of the Scripture passage has been fully discovered, the next responsibility of the sermonizer is to
draw out its applications. What vital bearings of truth
on the lives of his hearers flow out of this text as he now

thoroughly understands it? These applications should be logical deductions from the interpretation of the text. The expositor is an exporter of what is in the text actually and logically, not an importer of foreign material.

The Word of God has no meaning at all for practical life if it cannot be applied logically, cogently, and plainly as it stands. While the Holy Spirit alone can make the Word of God quick and powerful and sharper than any two-edged sword (Heb. 4:12), yet the preacher can be the Holy Spirit's instrument in applying the Word.

Many Scripture texts have direct application. They have been written or spoken directly to us. Others have indirect applications, having been written for us but not to us. Much of the historical material of the Bible was written about the Jews, or about Christ and the apostles, and thus must be indirectly applied to people today. The possibilities of indirect application are almost limitless. Dr. L. Berkoff writes:

The Bible as the Word of God contains a fulness and wealth of thought that is unfathomable. This is evident not only from its types and symbols and prophecies, but also from what it contains implicitly rather than by express assertion.[6]

Great care must be exercised in drawing applications or implications from Scripture passages. The *typical* method of interpreting the Old Testament has

6 L. Berkoff, *Principles of Biblical Interpretation* (Baker Book House, Grand Rapids 6, Mich., 1950), p. 157.

New Testament sanction, but should be kept within the bounds of legitimate types.[7]

Several commonly used methods of making applications are not to be commended. The *allegorical* method finds hidden meanings in the Scripture, and often these are valued above the contextual-grammatical-historical meanings. The *spiritualizing* method is akin to the allegorical. It finds devotional and inspirational meanings down underneath the literal meanings of passages. The *suggestive* method brings out various kinds of meanings or thoughts merely suggested by the text but which are not actually taught in it.

Some preachers find it easier to build up material by these questionable methods than by hard study, clear thinking, and careful spiritual deduction. And some congregations have heard so much allegorical, spiritualizing, suggestive preaching that they have come to think it more scholarly and spiritual than careful interpretation. Bernard Ramm[8] claims that the historic Protestant method of Bible interpretation is the literal-cultural-critical method, by which he means the same as our contextual-grammatical-historical method.

All methods of interpreting the Scriptures should earnestly seek to unfold their true meaning, magnify the Word of God, and glorify the Christ of God, not glamorize the cleverness and ingenuity of the preacher.

[7] For a fuller discussion of preaching on types, see F. D. Whitesell, *Evangelistic Preaching and the Old Testament* (Moody Press, Chicago, 1947), chap. III.

[8] Bernard Ramm, *Protestant Biblical Interpretation* (W. A. Wilde Company, Boston, 1950).

With the groundwork of interpretation and application thoroughly done, the preacher is now ready to arrange his material into sermonic form and perfect it into a message worthy of the Bible and the Christian pulpit.

REFERENCES

Homiletics

Berkhof, L., *Principles of Biblical Interpretation,* Grand Rapids: Baker Book House, 1950.

Blackwood, Andrew Watterson, *The Preparation of Sermons,* Nashville: Abingdon-Cokesbury Press, 1948.

Breed, David Riddle, *Preparing to Preach,* New York: George H. Doran Company, 1911.

Broadus, John A., *On the Preparation and Delivery of Sermons,* New York: Harper & Brothers, 1944, Part I, Chapter 2.

Etter, J. W., *The Preacher and His Sermon,* Dayton, Ohio: United Brethren Publishing House, 1891.

Garvie, Alfred Ernest, *The Christian Preacher,* New York: Charles Scribner's Sons, 1921.

Hoppin, James M., *Homiletics,* New York: Dodd, Mead and Company, 1881.

Kidder, Daniel P., *A Treatise on Homiletics,* New York: Carlton and Lanahan, 1866.

Pattison, T. Harwood, *The Making of the Sermon,* Philadelphia: The American Baptist Publication Society, 1898.

Tenney, M. C., *Galatians, The Charter of Christian Liberty,* Grand Rapids: Wm. B. Eerdmans Publishing Company, 1950.

Thomas, W. H. G., *Methods of Bible Study*, London: Thomas Marshall Brothers, 1903.
Torrey, R. A., *How to Study the Bible for Greatest Profit*, New York: Fleming H. Revell Company, 1896.

V

Vary the Propositions, Key Words and Transitions of Your Sermons

---

The integrating center of a sermon is a good proposition. The proposition promotes stability of structure, unity of thought and forcefulness of impact. The proposition is the heart of the sermon; in fact, it is the sermon in a nutshell, the gist of the sermon in a single sentence. Its importance for the sermonizer and for the audience can hardly be exaggerated.

This chapter purposes to show the homilist various methods of formulating and using this single idea on which the framework of the sermon is built.

THE NATURE OF PROPOSITIONS

In order to understand the nature of a proposition, we shall consider what various authorities have said about the proposition, and particularly the definitions they have given.

Ebenezer Porter, who, in 1834, wrote the first homiletics textbook in America, states that the proposition is an assemblage of words in which the theme of the discourse is announced. Bishop Whately suggests that it signifies a sentence in which something is said, affirmed or denied of another. It is that part of the sermon in which the theme is formally announced.

William G. T. Shedd, in his *Homiletics and Pastoral Theology*, 1876, states that the proposition is the enunciation of truth to be established and applied. Bishop Wilson T. Hogue wrote *A Handbook of Homiletics and Pastoral Theology* in 1886 in which he asserted that the proposition is that part of a sermon in which the theme is formally announced. He declares that the proposition should consist of only one such idea.

Austin Phelps, perhaps the outstanding champion of the proposition, in his notable work, *The Theory of Preaching*,[1] 1881, devotes eighty-two pages to this part of the sermon. He says that the proposition is that part of the discourse by which the subject is defined. It is a statement of the theme in sentence form. The elements of the proposition should be so related to each other that they are susceptible of unity of discussion. A proposition is a promise.

The latest revision of John A. Broadus' famous text, *On the Preparation and Delivery of Sermons*, 1944, asserts that the proposition is the gist of the sermon, a truth to be explained, appraised and applied.

G. W. Hervey, in *A System of Christian Rhetoric for the Use of Preachers and Other Speakers*, 1873, affirms that the proposition is the statement of the subject of a sermon or of the doctrine of its text. It is the ultimate conclusion to be established.

[1] This book of 588 pages was condensed and revised in 1947 by F. D. Whitesell and published by William B. Eerdmans Publishing Company, Grand Rapids, as a book of 167 pages.

James M. Hoppin of Yale, in his *Homiletics,* 1881, says that the proposition is that portion of the sermon in which the subject or the theme of the sermon is more distinctly and formally announced.

Herrick Johnson, in *The Ideal Ministry,* 1908, writes that the proposition answers the question, "What am I going to talk about?" Ozora Davis, in *Principles of Preaching,* 1924, indicates that the proposition is the statement, in its concisest form, in a complete sentence, of the theme that is to be discussed.

M. Reu, the Lutheran author of *Homiletics,* 1924, observes that the proposition is the formulated unity of the sermon, while Andrew W. Blackwood, in *The Preparation of Sermons,* 1948, declares that the proposition refers to a declarative sentence that contains the substance of the discourse.

In an eclectic approach to the definition of a proposition, it is wise not only to check the suggestions of homiletical authorities but also those of writers in the field of secular public speaking.

Thomas Wilson (1525–1581), the writer of the first comprehensive rhetoric in the English language, *Arte of Rhetorique,* 1560, teaches that there are seven parts of a speech: entrance, narration, proposition, division, confirmation, confutation, and conclusion. He explains the proposition as being "a pithie sentence comprehending in a small room the sum of the whole matter." We cite this definition because of its historical significance in the development of the idea of the proposition in secular rhetoric.

In surveying modern books in public speaking the

reader must be certain to understand the terminology used. Dr. Bess Sondel of the University of Chicago, in her work entitled *Are You Telling Them?* 1947, calls the proposition the controlling assertion. Gilman, Aly, and Reid, in *The Fundamentals of Speaking*, 1951, refer to the statement as "the formal phrasing of the central idea," while Bryant and Wallace, in *The Fundamentals of Public Speaking*, 1947, designate the proposition as the subject sentence. This last-named book shows the nature of the proposition in the following statement:

The subject sentence should clearly and completely state the theme or governing idea of the speech; in other words it should characterize or epitomize the ideas that you select to accomplish the purpose of the speech.[2]

These authors assert that this subject sentence should normally appear in the outline between the introduction and the development.

The preceding material on the proposition can be summarized by saying that the proposition of a sermon is a simple sentence stating the theme in proper form to be amplified, explained or proved; it is that statement of the theme in sentence form which the preacher proposes to develop and apply in his sermon.

THE CHARACTERISTICS OF PROPOSITIONS

The fundamental characteristics of a good proposition are unity, accuracy, clarity, brevity, universality and profitableness. The proposition should have *unity*.

[2] Bryant and Wallace, *Fundamentals of Public Speaking* (D. Appleton-Century Company, Inc., 1947), p. 228.

This unity can be gained by making certain that it is a simple sentence having but one subject, seeking but one aim, making but one impression. It should be *accurately stated*. *Accuracy, clarity* and *brevity* will be realized by the right arrangement of the fewest possible, simple, short, accurate words. All technical and figurative terminology, all synonyms and dangling phrases, should be avoided. The *universality* of the proposition stems from its statement of a timeless Biblical truth.

A proposition is *profitable* both for God and the listener when it states a scriptural truth pertinent to life's problems. The preacher is a spokesman for God and he most pleases God when he formulates propositions consisting of timeless, universal, significant Biblical truths. If the proposition is to be profitable to the listener, it should be based on a theme worthy of the listener's time to consider. There is little place for preaching on minor themes, especially when we remember that an audience of five hundred people listening to a thirty-minute message spends a total of two hundred and fifty hours of time on that one message. This fact alone should impel a preacher to make certain that he has a profitable proposition for the listener. A good proposition, logically developed, controls the flow of supporting material, excluding the irrelevant and utilizing the relevant.

VARIETY IN OBTAINING PROPOSITIONS

The first method suggested for formulating a proposition is that of *a limited definition of the subject*. Bryant and Wallace write:

Try to formulate a *limited* definition; i.e., in your subject sentence point out *one important way* in which your subject—whether it deals with an object, a play, a novel, a process, a mechanism, a word, a person, or an institution — is also distinguished from other closely related subjects.[3]

For example, faith is taking God at His word.

The second method of formulation might be termed the *purposive method*. In this the preacher states his proposition in sentence form and includes a statement of either the general or specific purpose behind his message. Sarett and Foster say:

Usually the speaker should phrase in one sentence, if possible, the special issue, the central idea, or the specific response that he seeks.[4]

Gilman, Aly, and Reid agree that the statement should be worded to accomplish not only a general purpose but also a specific purpose if there is one. They write:

Instead of saying, "The need for safety in industry has increased," when your specific purpose is to persuade your hearers to protect themselves, you should phrase your statement, "The workers in this plant should use the prescribed safety equipment."[5]

When the proposition is formulated in this purposive fashion, it will normally include either a "must" or a "should."

[3] Bryant and Wallace, *idem.*, p. 216.
[4] Sarett and Foster, *Basic Principles of Speech*, p. 410.
[5] Gilman, Aly, and Reid, *Speech Preparation* (Artcraft Press, Columbia, Mo., 1946), p. 50.

A third method of formulating a proposition might be called *the summary method.* This proposition includes not only the simple statement of the theme but also the announcement of the main points of the message. Such a proposition would not normally be advisable, since it eliminates the element of anticipation on the part of the audience. When the speaker reveals his complete development at the beginning, he loses the benefit of the surprise factor as he proceeds from point to point. However, this summary method may be advisable when the teaching aim is predominant, or when the material is difficult, or when the announcement of the points arouses curiosity as to their development.

VARIETY THROUGH THE SENTENCE
STRUCTURE OF PROPOSITIONS

The common sentence form used for the proposition is the simple declaration. This might be called *the declarative proposition.* It is a clear, concise statement of the theme in declarative form, e.g., "Prayer brings many benefits."

A second type of propositional sentence form is the interrogation. Such might be termed an *interrogative proposition.* This asks a question or poses a problem, e.g., "What are the benefits of prayer?"

The proposition may also be stated in the form of an exhortation. This is termed a *hortatory proposition.* The theme of the sermon is set forth in such a fashion that it exhorts the listeners to follow the prescribed suggestion, e.g.; "Keep on praying."

When the proposition is stated as an exclamation it is an *exclamatory proposition,* e.g., "Think of the many benefits of prayer!"

VARIETY BY DIFFERENT FORMS OF
ANNOUNCING THE PROPOSITION

Not only should the form of the proposition be diversified, but it should be announced in various ways. Thus the members of the congregation are not able to detect the bony structure of the sermon as easily. The following suggestions are a few of the many phrasings that may introduce the proposition:

I invite your attention . . .
I propose to speak . . .
I aim to prove . . .
My intention is to illustrate . . .
The text suggests . . .
The text is an example of . . .
My desire is to consider . . .
This message will be devoted to . . .
The service of this hour will consider . . .
Our common experience emphasizes . . .
Let us consider this truth . . .

A skilful use of these and other statements of introduction will serve to announce to the congregation this most important foundational element of the sermon, the proposition.

VARIETY THROUGH THE USE OF DIF-
FERENT METHODS OF TRANSITION

When the speaker has formulated his theme in propositional form, his next problem is to break it down into main points for logical discussion. This is most skilfully done by using an interrogative adverb and a key word. The interrogative serves as a directional marker setting forth the pathway of the message, and leads to the choice of the key word which characterizes or classifies the main points.

The transitional sentence incorporates the proposition, the key word and the interrogative idea into a smooth sentence, making the transition from the introduction to the main points. This process may seem mechanical, and, in a measure, it is, but it is essential to clarity of thought, smoothness of development, and homiletical efficiency. We must remember that, while the secular public speaker speaks occasionally, the pulpiteer speaks several times each week and must economize his time and energy. Therefore, he should have an efficient process for "prying out" a message.

One of the most commonly used interrogatives is "Why?" If the proposition of the sermon is "Every Christian should testify for Christ," the application of this interrogative would make it read, "Why should every Christian testify for Christ?" The homilist then proceeds to choose a plural noun which will answer this question. The noun, "reasons," seems to be the best one in this case. This is his key word, and every main point must be a reason why a Christian should testify for Christ. The speaker then formulates a transitional sentence comprised of three parts: the proposition, the interrogative idea, and the key word, resulting in this: "There are many reasons why a Christian should testify for Christ." He is now ready to state his first main point, the first reason.

The key word is always a plural noun which characterizes the main points. The following are a few of the many key words:

abuses	barriers	challenges
actualities	beginnings	changes
accusations	beliefs	charges
admonitions	benefits	circumstances
affairs	bequests	commands
affirmations	bestowments	commitments
agreements	blemishes	comparisons
alternatives	blessings	conceptions
angles	blows	concessions
answers	blockades	corrections
applications	blots	criteria
approaches	blunders	criticisms
areas	boasts	crowns
arguments	bonds	cults
aspects	books	cultures
aspirations	boundaries	customs
assertions	breaches	
assurances	burdens	
assumptions		dangers
attitudes	calls	debts
attributes	categories	decisions
avocations	causes	declarations
axioms	certainties	deeds
		deficiencies

definitions
degrees
departments
details
differences
directives
disciplines
disclosures
discoveries
divisions
doctrines
doubts
doors
dreams
duties

editions
effects
elements
encouragements
examples
excesses
exchanges
exclamations
experiments
explanations
exponents
exposures
expositions
expostulations
expressions
extremes

facets
facts
factors
faculties
failures
falls
families
faults
fears
feelings
fields
finalities
flaws
forces
forms
formalities
foundations
functions
fundamentals

gains
generalizations
gifts
graces
groups
guarantees
guides

habits
handicaps
honors
hopes
hungers

hurts

ideas
ideals
idols
ills
illuminations
illustrations
imitations
impacts
impediments
imperatives
imperfections
implements
implications
impossibilities
impressions
improvements
inadequacies
incentives
incidents
injunctions
invitations
irritations
issues
items

joys
judgments
justifications

keys
kinds

labors
lapses
laws
leads
lessons
levels
liabilities
liberties
lifts
lights
limits
links
lists
loads
locations
looks
losses
loyalties

manifestations
manners
marks
materials
means
measures
meetings
members
memories
mentions
mercies
methods
ministries
miseries

misfortunes
mistakes
models
moods
motives
mountains
movements
mysteries

names
narratives
natures
necessities
needs
nights
norms
notes
numbers

objects
objectives
obligations
observances
observations
obstacles
occasions
occurrences
offenses
offers
offices
omissions
operations
opinions

opponents
options
orders
organizations
origins

panaceas
parables
paradoxes
paragraphs
parallels
particulars
parties
parts
paths
patterns
peaks
peculiarities
penalties
perceptions
perfections
performances
perils
periods
perplexities
persons
personalities
petitions
phases
philosophies
phrases
pictures
pieces

places
plagues
plans
pleas
pledges
plots
points
positions
possibilities
powers
practices
prayers
precautions
predicaments
predictions
premises
preparations
prescriptions
pressures
pretensions
principles
privileges
prizes
problems
processes
products
profits
prohibitions
promises
proofs
prophecies
propositions
prospects

provisions
punishments
purposes
pursuits

qualifications
qualities
quantities
queries
quests
questions
quotas
quotations

ranks
ratings
reactions
reasons
recommendations
records
recruits
references
regions
regulations
rejections
relapses
relations
responses
restraints
results
revelations
rewards
roads

rôles
roots
routes
rules

sacrifices
satisfactions
sayings
scales
scars
schools
schemes
seals
seasons
secrets
selections
sentiments
sequences
services
shields
situations
skills
solicitations
solutions
sources
spheres
states
statements
steps

stipulations
stresses
strokes

styles	tones	ventures
subjects	topics	verifications
sufferings	traces	views
superlatives	traits	violations
suppositions	treasures	virtues
superiorities	trends	visions
supports	trials	vocations
symptoms	triumphs	voices
systems	troubles	
		wants
tactics	truths	warnings
talents	types	ways
tasks		weaknesses
teachings	uncertainties	weapons
tendencies	undertakings	words
tests	units	works
theories	urges	worries
theses	uses	wrongs
thoughts		
ties	vacancies	yieldings
times	values	yokes
titles	variations	
tokens	varieties	zones

Some suggestions can be given to help in the choice of the interrogative to be applied to a given proposition. The five useful interrogatives are: "What?" "Why?" "How?" "When?" "Where?" Only one interrogative should be used in any sermon. To use more than one confuses the principle of division, makes the selection of a key word virtually impossible, and broadens the scope of discussion beyond proper limits.

The preacher will doubtless use the interrogatives,

"Why?" and "How?" more frequently than others. "Why?" suggests reasons and "How?" suggests ways or methods. In most cases we will wish to give reasons why a thing should be done, or why it is true; or we will desire to suggest ways or methods of doing it. Instead of always using the interrogative, "Why?" in the transitional sentence the preacher may use, "because of." This phrase is followed by such phrases as: "benefits derived," "possibilities realized," "results produced," "honors won," "challenges offered."

When the interrogative, "How?" is applied to the proposition, it will help in the transitional sentence to use the preposition, "by," in conjunction with a verbal, e.g., "By following Christ's instructions a Christian may become an effective soul-winner." Other suggested combinations, using "by" plus a gerund, would include: "by following injunctions," "by observing principles," "by surmounting obstacles," "by overcoming barriers."

If the interrogative applied to the proposition is, "Where?" a key word denoting location will be demanded. In order to use such a key word in combination with the proposition within the transitional sentence, we advise that either the phrase, "at which" or "in which," be used in place of the original interrogative, "Where?" For example, "There are numerous areas *in which* Christians are needed for testifying." Other suggested key words to be used with this interrogative would include: places, situations, positions, circumstances, areas, regions, conditions, states, cities, organizations.

The interrogative, "When?" will be asked when

the proposition denotes a series of times. Such a time sequence used in the development of the message might include: morning, noon, and night; spring, summer, fall, and winter; past, present, and future; e.g., "When is the time to pray?" or "When should a church engage in evangelism?"

If the simple subject or predicate noun of the proposition is a collective noun, the interrogative, "What?" will function best. This interrogative introduces a key word denoting classification, such as the following: types, kinds, modes, categories, departments, divisions, varieties, and variations.

This method of bringing variety through the use of different interrogatives to formulate the transitional statement is not a revised version of the so-called "adverbial method" of earlier textbooks. That method suggests that a different interrogative be used to obtain each main point of the message, e.g., in speaking on "Intercessory Prayer," the main points would be: (1) What is it? (2) Why should it be practiced? (3) Who should do it? (4) When should it be done? (5) Where is the place to do it? (6) What results will be forthcoming? This method takes the speaker over an area too broad for satisfactory discussion in one sermon.

How much better it would be to take the theme of "Intercessory Prayer" and limit it by proposition, e.g., "Intercessory prayer is a Christian duty." The interrogative, "Why?" enables us to give a series of reasons why intercessory prayer is a Christian duty. Or we could use the proposition, "Every Christian can be effective in intercessory prayer." Then the interrogative,

"How?" would be the proper one to use. We would ask, "How can every Christian be effective in intercessory prayer?" The answer would give us the key word, "ways" or "methods." These suggested handlings narrow the theme of discussion, and thus promote clarity, vividness, depth of impression, practical application, and ease of development.

VARIETY THROUGH VARYING USES OF THE PROPOSITION

The proposition should always appear in the preparatory outline of the sermon. One of its primary uses is to stimulate and guide the homilist as he proceeds to amplify his theme. While it should always appear in sermon preparation, it need not appear formally every time in sermon presentation, but it should be strongly implied. Occasionally, the proposition can be taken for granted in the actual delivery of the sermon. The preacher will be so thoroughly saturated with his theme, and will have his material so logically arranged, that the proposition will be self-evident to the listener without specific declaration.

The normal position, or location, of the proposition, in both sermon preparation and presentation is at the close of the introduction. Another possibility is to withhold the proposition until the sermon is summarized at or near the close. This last suggestion helps when speaking to a hostile audience. In that case, the main points can lead up to, and lay the groundwork for, the proposition. For example, in preaching on the theme of the "Second Coming of Christ" to an audience hostile to the idea of His personal, visible and glorious return, the speaker might show: 1) That the world needs peace; 2) that the world needs justice, 3) that the world needs unification, 4) that the world needs competent leadership, and, in conclusion and as the proposition, "All these needs of the world will be met in the personal, visible and glorious return of Jesus Christ to this earth."

We give below two examples of the ideas taught in this chapter.

Single verse sermon

> *Text:* "Marvel not that I say unto thee, ye must be born again" (John 3: 7).
>
> *Subject:* The New Birth.
>
> *Theme:* The Necessity of the New Birth
>
> *Proposition:* You must be born again.
>
> *Interrogative:* Why?
>
> *Transitional sentence:* There are at least three reasons why you must be born again.
>
> *Key word:* Reasons
>
> *Main points:* I. In order to see the kingdom of God (John 3: 3).
>
> II. In order to enter the kingdom of God (John 3: 5).
>
> III. In order to understand spiritual things (John 3: 6).
>
> *Title:* New Life for You

*   *   *   *   *   *   *

Paragraph sermon

> *Text:* If any of you lack wisdom, let him ask of God, that giveth to all men liberally, and

upbraideth not; and it shall be given him. But let him ask in faith, nothing wavering. For he that wavereth is like a wave of the sea driven with the wind and tossed. For let not that man think that he shall receive any thing of the Lord. A double minded man is unstable in all his ways (James 1:5–8).

Subject: Wisdom

Theme: Obtaining Wisdom

Proposition: Believers Can Obtain Wisdom

Interrogative: How?

Transitional sentence: By meeting three conditions believers can obtain wisdom.

Key word: Conditions

Main points: I. By recognizing that you lack it (v. 5).

II. By asking God for it (v.6).

III. By believing that you will receive it (vv. 6–8).

Title: God's Wisdom for Man's Asking

REFERENCES

Homiletics

Davis, Ozora S., *Principles of Preaching,* Chicago: University of Chicago Press, 1924, Part II, Chapter 4.

Hervey, George Winfred, *A System of Christian Rhetoric for The Use of Preachers and Other Speakers,* New York: Harper & Brothers, 1873, Part II, Chapter 1, Section 2.

Hogue, Wilson T., *Homiletics and Pastoral Theology,* Winona Lake, Indiana: Free Methodist Publishing House, 1949, Chapter 10.

Hoppin, James M., *Homiletics*, New York: Dodd, Mead and Company, 1881, Division 4, Section 16.

Phelps, Austin, *The Theory of Preaching*, London: Richard D. Dickinson, 1882, Lecture 20–25.

Vinet, A., *Homiletics or The Theory of Preaching*, New York: Ivison and Phinney, 1854, Part II, Chapter 4.

Speech

Bryant, Donald C., and Wallace, K. R., *Fundamentals of Public Speaking*, New York: Appleton-Century Company, 1947, Chapter 11.

Gilman, Wilbur E., Aly, Bower and Reid, Loren D., *The Fundamentals of Speaking*, New York: The Macmillan Company, 1951, Part II, Chapter 4.

Norvelle, Lee and Smith, R. G., *Speaking Effectively*, New York: Green and Company, 1948, Part I, Chapter 1.

VI

Vary the Supporting Material in Your Sermons

Authorities on homiletics call this the process of development. It is simply expanding the outline into a fully developed sermon. Every point in the outline will have to be supported by the best possible material. Phillips Brooks said:

The true way to get rid of the boniness of a sermon is not by leaving out the skeleton, but by clothing it with flesh.[1]

Austin Phelps says that the qualities of good development are unity, pertinency, completeness, conciseness, order and proportion.

Development concerns the fourth and sixth of the seven essentials of speech preparation given by Alan Monroe. The seven are:

1. Determining the purpose of the speech;
2. Analyzing the audience and the occasion;
3. Selecting and narrowing the subject;
4. Gathering the material;
5. Making an outline of the speech;

[1] Phillips Brooks, quoted by G. Campbell Morgan in *Preaching* (Fleming H. Revell Company, New York, 1937), p. 70.

6. Wording the speech;
7. Practicing aloud.[2]

In rhetoric this process is called "invention," and includes the production, selection and arrangement of materials. Broadus points out that three processes are absolutely necessary: acquisition, reflection, and exercise. In secular public speaking, this is the process of building up a point so that it has wholeness and integrity. We assume that the analyses of the background, text, and theme are already in hand.

TEN WAYS TO OBTAIN SUPPORTING MATERIAL

The authors believe that for thorough study the process of invention should be broken down into more activities than the three that Broadus suggests, so we discuss this part of sermon preparation under ten headings. The preacher should make good notes on the following ten procedures as he goes along.

1. *Recall what you already know.* Any preacher will know something about almost any Biblical theme and a great deal about many. He should make notes of what he already knows or can recall.

2. *Meditate over your material.* With something as a starting point, the mind will develop other ideas and suggestions. One should start preparation in plenty of time to allow the mind to work without being hurried or forced. A week is all too short a time to prepare sermons, to say nothing of waiting until a day or two

---

[2] Alan H. Monroe, *Principles and Types of Speech,* Revised (Scott, Foresman & Co., New York, 1935), p. 95.

before you preach. The more time the mind has in which to work, the more it will do.

3. *Read all you can on the theme.* The minister will go to his files, scrapbooks, commentaries, Bible dictionaries, lexicons, books of theology and sermons. He should read at least three or four commentaries on any text or Scripture passage. This will give the preacher enough points of view to enable him to do some straight thinking for himself.

4. *Talk to others about it.* A minister can often discuss a theme or text with some other minister, some student, or some of his spiritually minded people; yes, his wife may be able to give him some helpful suggestions. Talking about a theme will tend to clarify his own thinking and to fix his material in his mind.

5. *Listen to sermons and discussions on the theme.* He may have opportunity to hear some other minister preach on his chosen theme, or to listen to a radio sermon or discussion of it.

6. *Observe and note all the daily occurrences and facts that bear on the theme.* The round of pastoral work may allow the preacher to see some practical demonstration of the thing he is preaching about, or some lack of it, or some illustration which bears on it.

7. *Pray about it.* The Lord has promised heavenly wisdom for the asking, and the Holy Spirit is able to lead us into all truth if we submit ourselves humbly to God in believing prayer. If men prayed over their sermons as long as they prepared otherwise, their messages, doubtless, would be more powerful. Robert F. Horton, in the Yale lectures published in 1893, said:

The threefold way of receiving the word of the Lord is study, meditation, prayer — prayerful study, studious meditation, meditative prayer, and again, as the girdle that binds on all pieces of the armor, prayer, long secret pleadings, passionate and definite requests, firm and believing grasps of the handle which prayer presents.[3]

Thomas Armitage wrote:

Your sermons will do little good in the pulpit unless all the integrities and energies of your soul have been penetrated by heart-searching prayer in the study; and a sermon steeped in prayer on the study floor, like Gideon's fleece saturated with dew, will not lose its moisture between that and the pulpit.[4]

8. *Use your imagination.* This remarkable faculty of the human mind is one of the most potent factors in sermonizing if we will let it be. Imagination is the picture-making faculty of the mind, and is able to bring Bible events back to life. True imagination stays within the realm of possible facts, but fancy runs wild into the realm of the impossible and unreal. Avoid fancy but use your imagination.[5]

9. *Allow the subconscious mind to work.* When the conscious mind quits work then the subconscious takes over. This part of the mind is at work while we sleep. That is why solutions to problems, and items we have tried in vain to recall, often pop into our minds

[3] Robert F. Horton, *Verbum Dei, the Yale Lectures on Preaching* (The Macmillan Company, New York, 1893), p. 177.

[4] Thomas Armitage, *Preaching: Its Ideal and Inner Life* (American Baptist Publication Society, 1880), p. 170.

[5] Two helpful and delightful chapters on imagination in preaching are chap. V, part IV, *On the Preparation and Delivery of Sermons* by Broadus-Weatherspoon, 1944; and chap. XI, *In the Minister's Workshop*, by Halford E. Luccock (Abingdon-Cokesbury, New York, 1944).

after we are in bed or at a waking period in the middle of the night. If we divide sermon preparation into several periods rather than try to grind out a complete sermon at one sitting, we give the subconscious mind opportunity to help us and make our preparation easier and more satisfactory. If, instead of worrying about the coming sermon, we would read our material and meditate on it immediately before retiring, we would set this subconscious mind to work and utilize its potentialities.

10. *Write out your ideas in fullest detail.* Writing tends to put the mind into a creative mood and to clarify ideas. Professional writers find that the very act of writing helps them to get ideas. They may need to force themselves to write, feeling that their minds are empty, but as they write, other ideas come. Then putting your ideas into written form gives better opportunity to criticize, revise, clarify, and elaborate them.

We believe that all these ten creative activities will be useful in preaching, though one may not use all of them in any one sermon. However, the more of these processes we use in sermon preparation, the more varied the sermon material is likely to be.

TEN RHETORICAL PROCESSES TO USE IN
OBTAINING SUPPORTING MATERIAL

Now we pass on to the consideration of specific rhetorical processes, or language techniques, which go into literary production. Broadus discusses four rhetorical processes, which he names the functional elements of the sermon (what one does in the sermon), namely, explanation, argumentation, illustration, and application. Dr. Charles W. Koller lists the rhetorical processes as six, namely, narration, interpretation, illustration, application, argumentation, and exhortation. All of the essential rhetorical processes might be included and discussed under either of these classifications, but for our purpose of being explicit in demonstrating how variety may be attained in sermon-making, we propose to discuss them under ten headings.

1. *Narration.* This is the simplest and easiest of the ten rhetorical processes, since it involves giving only an account of or telling the story of events and experiences. Often narration of a Biblical passage is necessary in order to present it in its proper setting and to clarify it. Sarett and Foster say, "Narration, although for the most part neglected by inexperienced speakers, is now and then the most effective method of development of a speech."[6] Narration may take on the nature of explanation, but it need not go that far. In preaching on a dramatic event or occurrence, narration may compose the bulk of the sermon, but one needs to be careful not to be too long, too tedious, and too repetitious in narration.

2. *Explanation.* This involves all the processes needed to make the meaning of the passage clear. It rests heavily on good exegesis. Some passages need more explanation than others. Explanation includes definition, description, comparison, and contrast. Definition may be done by citing synonyms, by classification, by division, by etymology, by negation and by

---

[6] Sarett and Foster, *Basic Principles of Speech,* p. 434.

noting the context. People will appreciate nothing more than clear, accurate and brief explanations of the text and other supporting Biblical material.

3. *Argumentation.* Argumentation is reasoning or giving proofs, and is perhaps not done as much today as in the 19th century, when more polemical preaching was in vogue. However, the sermon still needs the support of sound argument. Sarett and Foster claim that we use the principles of argumentation: (1) by analysis and synthesis, (2) by reasoning and evidence.[7]

The technical forms of arguments as taught in the older homiletics books are seldom mentioned today. We may use these forms, but we do not give them their technical names of *a priori, a posteriori, a fortiori, reductio ad absurdum, ex concesso,* and *ad hominem.*

We are more familiar with the use of evidence or testimony as a form of argument. And we know how to reason logically from general principles to specific cases, or from specific cases to general principles. The argument from analogy is not as strong as some others, yet it can carry great weight if skilfully handled.

Many speakers use statistics to support their statements. Statistics help to clinch arguments if they are accurate, up-to-date, representative, cover a sufficient number of cases, and are presented graphically.

A popular and practical division of argument, following that of Aristotle, is given by Thonssen and Gilkinson[8] as logical proof, emotional proof, and ethical proof. Logical proof is the most important and

7 Sarett and Foster, *idem.,* p. 439.
8 Thonssen and Gilkinson, *Basic Training in Speech* (D. C. Heath & Company, Boston, 1947), pp. 315 ff.

"embraces the reasoned sequences through which a proposition is established or disestablished." Deduction, induction, analogy, and argument from instances come under this heading.

While emotional proof is not as strong as logical, yet many people respond to it. All appeals to hatred, reverence, love, patriotism, etc., utilize emotional proof. Ethical proof stems from the speaker himself, including such factors as his personality, his attitudes, his intelligence, his sincerity, his tact and similar qualities — qualities which create confidence and good will. It is always a factor for or against the speaker, whether or not he recognizes it.

4. *Quotation*. Good quotations are extremely valuable. They may be from the Bible, from historical figures, or from present-day leaders. The greater authority a person has in his field, the more weight a quotation from him will carry. Quotations should not be too long or too frequent. If they can be quoted verbally rather than read, so much the better. Books of quotations may give some help, but the better quotations come from one's own reading and hearing.[9]

5. *Interrogation*. The rhetorical question asked the audience, but expecting no particular answer, is a device commonly used by good speakers to arouse attention. "How did the dying thief get to heaven?" you may ask, without expecting the listeners to answer, but going ahead to give the answer yourself. The rhetorical question should not be used too often.

[9] We recommend *The Home Book of Quotations* by Stevenson, *The New Encyclopedia of Practical Quotations* by Hoyt and *Familiar Quotations* by John Bartlett.

6. *Exhortation*. This takes the form of an appeal directly to the audience, to urge, to advise, to invite, to caution earnestly, or to admonish urgently. Exhortation is always proper in the conclusion of a sermon, but may occur elsewhere, as long as it is not overdone. The preacher needs to beware of overusing the words "oh" and "beloved" in exhortations.

7. *Repetition*. Any important truth or idea needs to be repeated or restated in order to underscore and emphasize it. Radio announcers and advertisers take great pains at this point. Repetition is one of the strong features of oral style as against written style. It can become boring if not handled properly. An idea can be repeated in identical words if something intervenes, or it can be restated in other words immediately following the first statement. The theme of a sermon, or the proposition, can well be restated in connection with each main point and the conclusion.

8. *Application*. Application brings the truth to bear on the thought and conduct of the hearers. It focalizes the claims of truth, it makes the personal encounter, it shows how to make use of the truth, and persuades to vital response. Thus application is one of the most important elements of the sermon and preaching is practically useless without it. Hearers are able to make some applications for themselves, but many are not intellectually and spiritually alert enough to make the right application unless the preacher helps them to do it.

9. *Illustration*. This important rhetorical process cites examples and cases bearing directly on the point

under discussion. It gives concreteness, vividness, and life to the presentation. So important is this process that we are using a whole chapter later on to discuss it.

10. *Imaginary conversation.* Instead of talking about or describing a person, the preacher can imagine him present, and carry on a conversation with him. This is called apostrophe. D. L. Moody often used this method when preaching on Bible characters. He called them out on the platform and talked to them as if they were right there. Evangelist Merv Rosell throws many of his arguments into imaginary discussions or debates between himself and the sinner he seeks to win, or the Christian he wishes to lead to higher ground.

These ten rhetorical processes will go a long way toward giving the preacher variety in the contents and style of his preaching. He will need to use most, if not all, of these processes if he reaches the eight speech goals suggested by Oliver, Cortright and Hager:

1. Make it interesting.
2. Make it arresting.
3. Make it significant.
4. Make it familiar.
5. Make it convincing.
6. Make it attractive.
7. Make it inevitable.
8. Make it appealing.[10]

TEN SOURCES OF SUPPORTING BIBLICAL MATERIAL

Since the Bible is the main source of preaching material, we would direct attention to the sources of Biblical supporting material. We are considering here those sources which give us direct help on our Scripture text or passage.

---

[10] Oliver, Cortright, and Hager, *The New Training for Effective Speech,* p. 142.

1. *The Bible.* We need to go directly to our text in our study Bible, read it carefully as it is, read it repeatedly, and read it in its immediate and remote context; then as similar passages occur to us we should read them too, making notes of all the ideas that come to us. Other translations of our text will be of great help.

2. *The concordances.* A concordance will enable us to run down other occurrences of subject words and help us to find plenty of supporting passages. The large concordances like Young's *Analytical* or Strong's *Exhaustive* will also give us the original Hebrew or Greek text of Scripture words.

Topical textbooks go somewhat beyond the concordances in that they classify Scripture passages according to subjects and suggest divisions of the subject. Perhaps the best are Nave's *Topical Bible* and Hitchcock's *Topical Analysis of the Bible.* A shorter one is *The New Topical Text Book* with introduction by R. A. Torrey.

3. *The Bible dictionaries and encyclopedias.* These give excellent summaries and condensations of all the Biblical material concerning persons, places, events, Bible books and principal ideas, along with Scripture references. The preacher needs two or three of these such as *The International Standard Bible Encyclopedia,* the Gehman-Davis *Bible Dictionary, The Standard Bible Dictionary,* or Smith's *Bible Dictionary.*

4. *The grammatical aids.* Even if the preacher is not able to read the original Hebrew and Greek, he can

still get much help concerning the original of his text
if he consults word-study books and exegetical helps.
But the man who has a working knowledge of the
original languages should use it in the light of his
lexicons and grammars. Such sets as A. T. Robertson's
Word Pictures in the New Testament, Vincent's *Word
Studies,* Vine's *Expository Dictionary of New Testament Words,* and Wuest's Greek exegetical books on
the New Testament will give the preacher many helpful suggestions and word-pictures to concrete his message.

5. *The commentaries.* Most of the commentaries
give both exegetical material and interpretations, and
some add homiletical suggestions. The preacher needs
a good stock of commentaries. Most are helpful, but
those that dig deep into original meanings are better.
With two or three sets of commentaries like *The Pulpit
Commentary, Lange's Commentary, Jamieson, Faucett
and Brown's Commentary, Calvin's Commentaries,
The Biblical Illustrator,* or *The Preacher's Homiletical
Commentary,* plus an individual commentary or two
on each book of the Bible by men like G. Campbell
Morgan, F. B. Meyer, J. C. Ryle, Handley Moule, William R. Newell, H. A. Ironside, W. H. Griffith Thomas,
and Roy Laurin, the preacher is well equipped with
interpretative material. Two sets of much value on
the Bible, recently republished, are Ryle's *Expository
Thoughts on the Gospels* and Albert Barnes' *Notes on
the Old and New Testaments.*

6. *The Bible geographies.* When places and loca-

tions are involved, a good Bible atlas or geography is most helpful. George Adam Smith's *Historical Geography of the Holy Land,* or the older Thompson's, *The Land and the Book,* give much commentary material additional to maps. The most recent work in this area has been done by G. Ernest Wright and Floyd V. Filson.

7. *The archeological books.* Biblical archeology has done much to make the Bible a living book, and the preacher should avail himself of the best and most up-to-date literature in this field. J. P. Free's *Archæology and Bible History* and H. H. Halley's popular *Pocket Bible Handbook* give much help and suggest other literature in the field. Hardly anything will interest people more than archeological facts.

8. *The Bible histories.* These books give the history of the Bible in chronological order, with comments and interpretations. Edersheim, Smith, Maclear, and Blaikie are popular.

9. *The theological works.* Most sermons will involve theology, both systematic and Biblical. The great orthodox books of systematic theology and Biblical theology will deal with most of the important passages of the Bible, and will help to clarify and systematize any doctrinal discussion. These books make us alert to discern theological error and wrong interpretations. The theological works of Calvin, Strong, Hodge, Berkhof, Mullins, Chafer, Thiessen and Fitzwater are all good.

10. *The sermonic literature.* We believe this

rightly belongs last in literature to be consulted for
direct Biblical help, but to read a sermon on your
chosen text may give a strong stimulus. We should be
careful not to copy any other preacher's outline or
sermon as a whole, but we can legitimately borrow
ideas and illustrations if we give proper acknowledge-
ment. The sermonic commentaries are such as Alexander MacLaren's, Hastings', Spurgeon's, W. B. Riley's
B. H. Carroll's, Joseph Parker's, Harry A. Ironside's
volumes, and the Expositor's Bible. In addition to some
of these, the preacher will have his own collection of
sermon volumes to consult for help. These should be
indexed for ready reference.

No preacher will consult books in all ten of these
fields for help on every sermon, but he will certainly
profit if he makes himself familiar with each field and
learns to go to each according to his need.

TWENTY-FIVE EXTRA-BIBLICAL LITERARY SOURCES
OF SUPPORTING MATERIAL

(1) Hymns, (2) Current events in newspapers, magazines,
or via radio, (3) Biographies, conversion stories, deeper experiences, life problems, (4) History, (5) The classics, (6)
Psychology, (7) Missionary literature, (8) Devotional literature, (9) Science, (10) Poetry, (11) Fiction, (12) Art (painting, sculpture, music, drama), (13) Apologetics, (14) Com-
parative religions and the cults, (15) Ethics, (16), Economics, (17) Philosophy, (18) Education, (19) Law, (20) Medi-
cine, (21) Health, (22) Sociology, (23) Sports, (24) Nature
studies, (25) Government and politics.

A major problem is to sift the supporting material so as to exclude the inappropriate. A sermon cannot be a mass of heterogeneous details. Piles of building material at the right location do not constitute an office building. There must be selection, arrangement, and integration in building construction. So it is with the sermon.

REFERENCES

Homiletics

Blackwood, Andrew Watterson, *The Fine Art of Preaching*. New York: The Macmillan Company, 1937, Chapter 4.

Broadus, John A., *A Treatise on the Preparation and Delivery of Sermons*. New York, London: Harper & Brothers, 1944, Part III, Chapter 2.

Davis, Ozora S., *Principles of Preaching*. Chicago: University of Chicago Press, 1924, Part II, Chapter 8.

Etter, J. W., *The Preacher and His Sermon*. Dayton, Ohio: United Brethren Publishing House, 1891, Part 1, Chapter 3, Part 11, Chapter 9.

Kidder, Daniel P., *A Treatise on Homiletics*. New York: Carlton and Lanahan, 1866, Chapter 2.

Speech

Baird, C., and Knower, F. H., *An Introduction to General Speech*. New York: McGraw-Hill, 1949, Chapter 5.

Bryant, Donald C., and Wallace, K. R., *Fundamentals of Public Speaking*. New York: Appleton-Century Company, 1947, Chapters 8 and 9.

Monroe, Alan Houston, *Principles and Types of Speech*. New York: Scott-Foresman and Company, 1939, Chapter 9.

Soper, Paul Leon, *Basic Public Speaking*. New York: Oxford University Press, 1949, Chapter 4.

Williamson, Arleigh B., Fritz, Charles A., and Ross, Harold Raymond, *Speaking in Public*. New York: Prentice-Hall, Inc., 1948, Chapters 18 and 19.

VII

Vary the Illustrations in Your Sermons

We cannot overemphasize the value of good sermon illustrations. Our generation is becoming more and more picture-minded. Rapid advances in all branches of photography are responsible for more and better pictures in the newspapers and magazines. The picture magazines, motion pictures, television, and all kinds of visual aids are steadily turning the educational process into one of visualization.

The increasing dependence on pictures to convey ideas tends to make us more passive and less inclined to do hard abstract thinking. Therefore, even more than in previous times, the preacher must employ more high-quality illustrations if he is to reach this restless, picture-minded age.

Psychology informs us that knowledge is obtained through our five senses in about the following ratios: sight, 85 per cent.; hearing, 10 per cent.; touch, 2 per cent.; smell, 1½ per cent., and taste, 1½ per cent. Sermon illustrations are mental pictures and tend to bring knowledge through the sense of sight.

Since most of the great preachers of the past have been adept users of illustrations, the modern preacher must give careful study to the art of illustrating and be continually on the watch for apt illustrations.

In a recent book F. D. Whitesell says:

The illustrations in Talmage's sermons were perhaps their most striking feature. He often used an illustration to begin a sermon, as does C. E. Macartney today. Henry Drummond's illustrations were always simple and natural. Phillips Brooks was always seeking to tell a story. Every sermon he preached was quivering with personal life. Spurgeon had a genius for illustration. His illustrations were often homely, sometimes daring, always realistic. Moody's sermons abounded in illustrations, and evangelistic preachers still quote his illustrations. Joseph Parker excelled in the power to use historical illustrations. Robert South was outstanding in the use of historical and Scriptural illustrations, and Beecher claimed an indebtedness to him. Frederick W. Robertson was not copious in the use of illustrations but used them effectively. W. B. Riley compiled eighty-three scrapbooks of illustrations and ideas over a period of sixty years. . . . He said they were a never failing source of help to him. George W. Truett's illustrations were deeply emotional and moving. Dr. Walter A. Maier, formerly of the Lutheran Hour, used illustrations freely but carefully. He checked the accuracy of every illustration down to the last detail, for if anything was wrong, some radio listener was bound to take him to task.[1]

We have already referred to illustration as one of the ten rhetorical processes for developing supporting material for the sermon, but because of its supreme importance, we have left its full discussion for this chapter.

[1] F. D. Whitesell, *The Art of Biblical Preaching* (Zondervan, Grand Rapids, 1950), pp. 92–93.

VARY THE PURPOSES OF ILLUSTRATIONS

The main thought most of us have in using illustrations is *to illuminate the subject*, and this purpose
is important. Blackwood declares that the purpose of
the illustration is to "make facts shine."[2] Carlyle says
about the illustrative portion of a sermon: "Always
throwing light upon the matter—that is the only part of
the speech worth hearing."[3]

Many have rightly likened illustrations to windows which admit light. In fact, the etymology of the
word "illustrate" means "to throw light upon." Every
building needs several windows, but a house is more
than windows. The windows should be obsolutely
transparent, for if they be stained windows they color
the light and attract attention to themselves, which is
not the purpose of illustrations.

Another purpose of illustrations is *to give wings
to speech* so that it may rise above the level of abstraction to that of objectivity. Good illustrations lift the
sermon into the heavenlies. Wilder Smith has written:

We might call them [illustrations] the wings of a speech,
sustaining and directing its flight. On them the thought
flies to any elevation and easily maintains itself there.[4]

A primary purpose of illustrations is *to obtain and
hold interest*. A listless audience can be easily and

2 A. W. Blackwood, *The Fine Art of Preaching* (The Macmillan Company, New York, 1943), p. 59.
3 William Evans, quoted by, *How to Prepare Sermons and Gospel Addresses* (Moody Bible Institute Colportage, Chicago, 1913), p. 135.
4 Wilder Smith, *Extempore Preaching* (Brown and Gross, Hartford,
Conn., 1884), p. 59.

quickly aroused to the point of complete attention by the use of a telling illustration. W. B. Riley says:

As fox hunters thrill to the voice of hounds when by their louder and more rapid barking they indicate that the trail has become fresher and hotter, so an audience responds to a vivid illustration of truth with awakened interest.[5]

Once interest is secured then the message can go back to more abstract discussion, but not for long. Another illustration will be necessary to hold the attention once secured. Many preachers believe it is well to use an illustration in the introduction. Dr. Clarence E. Macartney often does this. Thomas Guthrie (1803–1873), the great Scotch preacher, experimented to see how his people remembered by preaching sermons full of illustrations and others barren of illustrations. So convinced of the value and power of illustrations was he that he became one of Scotland's greatest illustrators. T. H. Pattison writes of him:

A painter among preachers, as he describes himself, Guthrie's pictures were often arguments. . . . Few men understood as well as did he the power of a fitting illustration, and no preacher of all time has told stories in sermons with greater effect. His world was full of pictures, and every truth to him was concrete or it was nothing.[6]

Also the right illustration at the beginning of a message may serve *to establish rapport with the audience.* Henry Ward Beecher said that one of the purposes of illustration was to employ tact, by which he meant

[5] W. B. Riley, *The Preacher and His Preaching* (Sword of the Lord Publishers, Wheaton, 1948), p. 114.
[6] T. Harwood Pattison, *The History of Christian Preaching* (American Baptist Publication Society, 1909), p. 326.

to set the speaker on good terms, or in sympathy, with his audience. This is especially true when the audience is strange or hostile.

Illustrations tend *to rest the audience* from close attention, and to relax them when the speaker has been particularly intense or abstract. The average hearer must have a rest at least about every five minutes. A bit of humor or light illustrative material will be appreciated for this very purpose.

Clarification of a subject is a purpose for illustrations closely akin to illumination. Broadus makes clarity the first essential of good style. Of all public speakers, the minister, above all others, should seek to be clear because of the importance of his message and its possible effects in time and eternity. One of the ways of explanation is to illustrate, or cite examples. Broadus says:

Exemplification is often necessary and almost always useful in the work of explanation. . . . To the most cultivated thinkers an idea will become more vivid and interesting when there is added to a precise definition some opposite example.[7]

Former President F. D. Roosevelt's speeches well illustrate this principle. In seven of his speeches, which have been carefully studied, he used seventy-two general examples, fifty-three specific examples and two hypothetical cases, or one hundred twenty-seven in all.[8]

Again, good illustrations *make truth vivid,* and vividness is one of the most desirable qualities of speech.

[7] Broadus, *The Preparation and Delivery of Sermons,* p. 165.
[8] Oliver-Dickey-Zelko, *Communicative Speech* (Dryden Press, New York, 1949), p. 102.

A vivid thing is one strikingly alive, or full of life. Franklin Fisk has written:

A good illustration can breathe life into dead thoughts so that the whole sermon shall pulsate with life. . . . If it stands forth like the sun, it will have the sun's power.[9]

Illustrations *strengthen argument*. Illustrations are not the best proof for an argument, and certainly ought not to be used as the only proof, yet the fact remains that in the minds of many hearers apt illustrations and examples do much to clinch an argument. The examples of faith in Hebrews 11 go far to strengthen the writer's argument for the primacy of faith in the spiritual life.

Then illustrations can be used *to bring conviction of sin*. If one were preaching against covetousness he would hardly omit the two Biblical illustrations of Achan in the Book of Joshua and Ananias and Sapphira in the Book of Acts. The illustration of the rich fool from Luke 12 would also help to bring conviction. Many striking illustrations occur every day showing that the wages of sin is death.

Illustrations can be used *to persuade*. Sometimes, illustrations are more persuasive than argument. A striking illustration showing the benefits of an action, particularly in or near the conclusion of the sermon, followed by an earnest exhortation or appeal, will be powerfully persuasive. This applies especially to evangelistic preaching. Dr. W. B. Riley recommends the best illustration for the conclusion. He wrote:

[9] Franklin W. Fisk, *Manual of Preaching* (A. C. Armstrong & Son, New York, 1896), p. 256.

Scores of times within the sixty-three years of my ministry have I put in literally hours searching for that last illustration, knowing full well that upon its employment might depend not only the power of the sermon, but the destiny of immortal souls.[10]

Illustrations *aid the memory*. People are likely to remember the illustrations longer than anything else about the sermon. If illustrations are properly adjusted to the truth they illustrate, they carry some of that truth into the memory. Pictures are more likely to be remembered than abstract ideas, and good illustrations are verbal pictures.

Illustrations *can ornament* the sermon. The fitting illustration gives the sermon dress, balance, vigor and vividness, all of which tend toward sermon splendor or legitimate ornamentation.

Touches of humor can be injected by illustrations. Americans are eager for humor, and doubtless there is some place for a little of it in preaching, particularly when it comes naturally to the speaker. Pulpit humor, however, must be kept at a safe minimum and used with delicacy and good taste. No vulgar or carnal humor has any place in the Christian pulpit. Humor should not be an end in itself and should never rob a speaker of his control over his audience.

Illustrations *stimulate the hearers' imagination*. Imagination is a high type of thinking, and if something strikes the mind of the listener whereby he imagines himself a better man, or if his imagination shows him how to achieve a spiritual victory, he has been

10 W. B. Riley, *The Preacher and His Preaching*, p. 124.

helped. Since illustrations are pictures, they arouse the imagination more than any other part of the sermon.

A preacher *may speak indirectly through his illustrations* when it would not be wise to speak directly. If a pastor is plagued by church bazaars and other worldly practices of making money, a direct attack might prove fatal to his usefulness in that church, whereas, now and then, he might use an illustration of spiritual churches in which direct giving accomplishes more, and thus gradually create sentiment for his position. Henry Ward Beecher struck some telling blows against slavery in his illustrations without making a direct frontal attack on the institution. Then illustrations have a capacity to be applied in different ways by different auditors, each making an indirect application to his own need.

A speaker may use illustrations *to appeal to the children in his congregation.* Children may not be interested in doctrinal discussions or historical issues, but the minute lively illustrations are introduced the children begin to listen. Stories and anecdotes usually appeal to a child, and anything that interests the children will tend to interest adults too.

And, finally, illustrations *tend to make a message practical.* They show that the truths proclaimed are related directly to life. Mathewson insists that illustrations apply to life principles when he points out that:

1. Illustration exemplifies a certain principle.
2. Illustration helps one to see a principle in action.
3. Illustration aids in making the application.

4. Illustration helps to show the need or advantage of a certain principle.
5. Illustration helps to show the prevalence of a principle.
6. Illustration assists in showing the disastrous consequences of the failure of a principle.[11]

The speaker, then, may have in mind any one or more of a wide variety of purposes when he uses illustrations; and the fact that an illustration used for one purpose may accomplish a number of other good purposes, all goes to prove that every speaker must give great care in the selection, adjustment, and use of appropriate illustrations.

VARY THE TYPES OF ILLUSTRATIONS

Since the most popular concept of an illustration is that of a story, we shall begin with it.

1. *The story.* A story may be long or short, true or fictitious, but it is a connected narrative of some experience. It is the oldest type of literature, and there is an abundance of stories available. *Aesop's Fables* give one kind of useful story. Mythology provides us with many interesting stories. History, biography, drama, literature, all abound with stories to be discovered and used.

Jesus as a preacher and teacher was a supreme storyteller, while Abraham Lincoln, a secular speaker, had a large fund of appropriate stories. Jenkins says:

If a story is vital and pertinent in its portrayal of things that can be seen, felt, and touched, then it may bring the

11 Lester Mathewson, *The Illustration* (Fleming H. Revell Company, New York, 1936), p. 13 ff.

unseen eternal values so close that we can touch them with our finite minds.[12]

2. *Anecdotes.* An anecdote is a story either humorous or serious, usually with real life characters. It is usually brief, pointed, and interesting, sometimes with a touch of humor. The sayings and doings of children often fall into this classification.

3. *Parables.* Parables are stories of a particular type. A parable is a comparison or analogy, a short narrative from which a moral or spiritual truth is easily drawn. Jesus excelled in the use of parables. While He may not have been thinking about particular persons or events in each case, yet He was careful to use typical life situations to convey eternal truth.

4. *Object lessons.* These consist of some visible object, such as a pencil, a coin, a glass of water, some object or symbol that represents the truth being taught. Object lessons have been used with children almost exclusively, but there certainly is a proper place for the use of select object lessons in any pulpit. They are especially helpful as a means of persuading a believing audience.

5. *Dramatics.* This method of illustrating uses the idea of re-enacting the scene. Dr. J. M. Price says of it:

It is, therefore, primarily an imitative and reproductive activity. . . . So we think of it as the acting out of a truth or lesson, whether or not there is any definite basis of fact.[13]

[12] Leonard Rush Jenkins, *450 Stories from Life* (The Judson Press, Philadelphia, 1947), p. 13.
[13] J. M. Price, *Jesus the Teacher* (The Southern Baptist Convention, Nashville, 1946), p. 97.

Ezekiel was a great dramatic prophet and preacher. Stirring scenes and lively action stories tempt the speaker to dramatization. Dramatization is good if not carried to extremes and if done skilfully. The speaker's actions should not deflect the attention of the audience from the truth presented. One preacher was preaching about Jesus casting the demons out of the herd of swine. As he pictured them rushing down a cliff into the sea, he became so wrapped up in his dramatization that he jumped off the pulpit platform down into the audience, almost scaring some of the saints out of their wits. This was a good thing overdone.

6. *Allegories.* Allegories are sustained comparisons, or prolonged metaphors, in which one thing is presented under the image of another. Jesus' allegory of the vine and the branches in John 15 is a good New Testament example. Bunyan's famous *Pilgrim's Progress* is an outstanding extra-Biblical example.

7. *Figurative language.* This realm of illustration carries us all the way from the one-word illustration to the extended narrative. The *metaphor* is a common type of figurative language in which a word or phrase literally denotes one kind of object or idea in place of another by way of suggesting a likeness or analogy between them, e.g., the ship *plows* the sea.

The *simile* is a figure of speech directly expressing a resemblance in one or more points of one thing to another. Matthew 23:37 is a good example, "How often I would have gathered your children together as a hen gathers her brood under her wings, but ye would not."

The *hyperbole* is an obvious exaggeration for

effect. The *paradox* is a seeming contradiction. The *contrast* is a pointing out of differences.

8. *Poems.* Poetry is the language of imagination and emotion using the devices of rhyme, rhythm, and meter. We should use only that part of a poem illustrating the point and care should be taken not to use poetry excessively. Poetry quoted from memory will have the best effect.

9. *Analogies.* These point out likeness of relations, or the resemblance, not of the things themselves, but of two or more attributes, circumstances, or effects. Many non-narrative illustrations fall into this category, e.g., soul-winning is analogous to fishing in certain respects; the Gospel to dynamite; prayer to the radio.

10. *Quotations.* Direct quotations usually attract attention and are good to reinforce a point if they come from a recognized authority. Citing the name of the authority quoted helps to give the quotation color, force and authority. Writers are advised to use plenty of direct quotations for sake of reader interest.

The Biblical preacher, therefore, will wish to put variety into his sermons by varying the types of illustrations he uses.

VARY THE SOURCES OF ILLUSTRATIONS

The preacher should draw his illustrations from all possible sources. As he cultivates the homiletical mind, he will see many illustrations that he previously missed. In the following list of illustration sources, we have tried to list what we consider to be the better ones first:

1. *The Bible*. These excel all others but should not constitute the whole of one's illustrations.

2. *Personal experience*. These can always be told with power, providing the personal pronoun "I" is not used too often. Any sermon may contain two or three personal experience illustrations but should not go beyond that. Dr. C. W. Koller says that if the personal reference is justifiable the preacher need not say, "Pardon the personal reference." If the personal reference is not justifiable neither God nor man will pardon the preacher.

3. *Personal observation*. Illustrations of this class are things observed rather than experienced. The pastor will meet with many personal observations in his pastoral work, but must be careful not to use names, addresses, or definite identification marks. No pastor can afford to give his people the impression that personal confidences will ever become public property in this or any other pastorate. Observations of animals often make good illustrations.

4. *Inanimate nature*. Illustrations of growing things, trees, grass, flowers, garden produce, grain, all give many illustrations, as do rivers, mountains, the oceans, the plains, the stars, the clouds, sky, etc. Jesus was a prolific user of nature illustrations.

5. *Travel*. These illustrations may be personal observations, or experiences, or nature illustrations, but they are observed on travels and deserve a separate classification. Every time a preacher takes a trip he should be on the look-out for illustrations and record them in his notebook.

6. *Athletics.* Illustrations from this field will have to be culled so as not to reflect wordliness or the commendation of questionable practices, but some good illustrations can be gleaned from this field, and they will make a particular appeal to young people.

7. *Newspapers, magazines, radio and television.* These represent the reading and listening one does to keep up with the world.

8. *Biographies.* This is a special source of gems for the preacher. He should read many biographies and be careful to record the illustrations. F. A. Boreham's books, *A Bunch of Everlastings, A Basket of Cameos,* and *A Handful of Stars* are examples of how to use biographical illustrations.

9. *History.* Because it deals with events and people it gives many useful illustrations. Fogg's book of famous sayings of history is good.

10. *Missions.* The history of missions and the literature of missions contain many wonderful illustrations of Christian faith, suffering, and accomplishment. E. M. Harrison's missionary books give many excellent illustrations.

11. *General literature.* The classics, poetry, fiction, drama, all yield useful illustrations.

12. *Science.* Applied science is bristling with fine illustrations, but the preacher must be accurate and up to date and not weight his sermons too heavily with such references.

13. *Art.* The realms of painting, sculpture, music, drama and architecture, all yield good illustrations. We recommend W. E. Biederwolf's book of illustra-

tions from art, Cynthia Pearl Maus' *Christ and the Fine Arts,* and Albert Edward Bailey's books *The Gospel in Art* (1936), *Christ and His Gospel in Recent Art* (1948), and *The Gospel in Hymns; Backgrounds and Interpretation* (1950).

14. *Imagination.* Many illustrations can be imagined or invented. The danger the preacher must avoid is that of drawing too many illustrations from one source, e.g., his own family, fishing, the automobile, etc. Not only should he vary his illustrations over the course of a year's preaching, but he should vary them in every sermon. Nothing will help him get variety into his preaching more than this practice.

VARY THE NUMBER OF ILLUSTRATIONS

While it is good to follow Aristotle's advice of using one major illustration for every main point, yet this should not be the unalterable pattern. Since there are many types of illustrations, and so many sources of illustrations, as well as types of sermons, some sermons may be packed with illustrations, while others have relatively few. A biographical sermon, a parabolic sermon or a historical sermon would not need so many outside illustrations; but a doctrinal sermon, or an ethical sermon, should have more.

Some men feel that there is a danger in having too many illustrations—"just a string of stories" tied together, they say. We admit that this can happen. Such sermons may require but little preparation; but, on the other hand, we feel that the greater danger lies in not having enough illustrations. There should be depth, plenty of it; truth, volumes of it; doctrine, oceans of it; but all must be illustrated if it is to take hold of and transform lives.

Henry Ward Beecher was a great illustrator. He said: "I use fifty illustrations now to one in the early years of my ministry."

VARY THE TECHNIQUE OF ILLUSTRATING

We should avoid using a single technique in illustrating. We make the following suggestions:

1. *Vary the length of illustrations.* Beware of unusually long ones, but they can be used occasionally.

2. *Vary the method of emphasizing the lesson of the illustration.* Do not make this part too lengthy. Omit stating the lesson sometimes, and let the hearer make the application.

3. *Vary the terminology used in introducing illustrations,* e.g., "Let me illustrate"; "Now, for example"; "I am thinking of a person who"; "Consider this"; "Dr. Jowett tells the story of"; and "Emerson writes of." Avoid such clichés as "It is said"; and "They say." Sometimes you can use the illustration without any introductory words, particularly at the beginning of a sermon.

4. *Vary the emotional tone of illustrations.* Go from the doleful and sad to the bright and cheerful, from the light to the heavy. Avoid using all deathbed illustrations, all conversions, all consecrations, all fishing stories, all agricultural illustrations.

5. *Vary the age appeal of illustrations.* Have some-

thing dealing with the interests of children, high-school pupils, working men, housewives, old folks.

VARY THE MODELS YOU FOLLOW IN ILLUSTRATING

We do well to read and hear the sermons of great pulpit masters and learn how they use illustrations, but we should not follow the example of only one man. However, it is perfectly natural that we have one or two favorite preachers to whom we devote most attention.

George W. Truett was outstanding in the use of illustrations from his own personal experience. He knew how to use them without exalting himself. He exalted Christ to the highest heavens and powerfully moved his hearers in Christ's direction.

John Henry Jowett was an artist in the use of language and always had his illustrations skilfully adjusted to his message in the fewest possible words. He drew illustrations from everywhere, but, more than most preachers, he took illustrations from the field of preaching. He used very few personal illustrations.

Charles Haddon Spurgeon was an artist in his ability to use word pictures. With a highly developed but well-controlled imagination, he used similes and metaphors freely, and took most of his illustrations from the Bible and common life. He seldom used gripping contemporary stories.

F. W. Boreham is a master in the use of biographical illustrations. Out of some thirty books which he has produced, several of the most popular deal with the key texts of famous men. His sermons are not weighty but are full of human interest because they abound in illustrative material from biography, poetry, history, pastoral life, and personal experiences.

Clarence Edward Macartney, author of some forty books, is one of the best sermonic illustrators of our times. He has even published a book of sermon illustrations. He also uses many Bible illustrations and many from history and biography.

Clovis G. Chappell has produced about twenty-five books of sermons and Bible expositions. His main aim is to catch and hold interest, and to do this he uses many illustrations from the Scriptures and homely daily life. He seldom uses word pictures and poetry but he does speak plainly and makes smooth transitions from one illustration to another.

Adoniram J. Gordon was a spiritual preacher of first rank. He knew how to use simple illustrations effectively. His skill in making an illustrative incident apply pointedly seldom has been equaled. Always sweet, gentle, and full of grace, this man of God drew often on the Bible for illustrative material, but perhaps more often on the lives of the great spiritual giants of the past. His book, *The Two-Fold Life,* gives many experiences from the lives of people who pressed on to know the Lord in His fulness.

These men are only a few of the many who might be studied for guidance in the art of illustrating sermons. We would say that it is well to study the pulpit masters in addition to studying books of theory on how to do it.

We believe that books of sermon illustrations

should be avoided. When one is pressed for time he may find some help in such books and thus struggle to save his sermon, but to fall into the habit of continually leaning on these crutches is deplorable. Seldom can the preacher use these "canned goods" with real power. Perhaps the worst part about sermon illustration books is that their contents soon become public property and the preacher may be using some hackneyed old illustrations that his people already have heard a number of times.

A filing system for sermon illustrations is desirable. Dr. W. B. Riley used and recommends Todd's *Index Rerum*, an old system based on the vowels of the alphabet. Many commercial index systems are on the market. The preacher needs to take care not to start something that will be too complex and time-consuming to maintain. The authors would not care to suggest any particular system.

REFERENCES

Homiletics

Blackwood, Andrew Watterson, *The Preparation of Sermons.* Nashville: Abingdon-Cokesbury Press, 1948, Chapter 13.

Breed, David Riddle, *Preparing to Preach.* New York: George H. Doran Company, 1911, Chapter 14.

Broadus, John A., *A Treatise on the Preparation and Delivery of Sermons.* New York, London: Harper & Brothers, 1944, Part III, Chapter 3.

Bryan, Dawson C., *The Art of Illustrating Sermons.* Nashville: Cokesbury Press, 1938, 272 pp.

Gowan, Joseph, *Homiletics or The Theory of Preaching*. London: E. Stock, 1922, Chapter 10.

Pattison, T. Harwood, *The Making of the Sermon*. Philadelphia: The American Baptist Publication Society, 1898, Chapters 17 and 18.

Sangster, William Edwin, *The Craft of Sermon Illustration*. Philadelphia: Westminster Press, 1950, 125 pp.

Speech

Crocker, Lionel, *Public Speaking for College Students*. Chicago: American Book Company, 1941, Chapter 13.

Prochnow, Herbert Victor, *The Public Speaker's Treasure Chest*. New York: Harper & Brothers, 1942, 413 pp.

VIII

Vary the Arrangement of Material in Your Sermons

Proper arrangement of sermonic material is virtually as important as the material itself. The force and effectiveness of the material depends, in a large measure, on its orderly arrangement. A mere collection of material is not a sermon, but it is the intelligent and forceful arrangement of material that makes it a sermon. David R. Breed has rightly said:

A collection of ideas, however well they may be separately expressed, is no more a discourse than a collection of material, however good, is a building, or a company in uniform, however fine, is an army.[1]

In the same degree that good planning is necessary in architecture, in landscaping, in music, and in literature, so it is in sermon-making

Good arrangement is a powerful aid to both preacher and people. For the preacher, it stimulates thought, gives him confidence, accelerates his work, assists in working out details, helps his memory, enables him to make proper emphases, and causes his feelings to flow more freely. For the audience, good

[1] David R. Breed, *Preparing to Preach*, p. 65.

arrangement makes the material more intelligible, pleasing, interesting, persuasive and easily remembered. Earl W. Wells, in *The Quarterly Journal of Speech*,[2] says that good organization of material removes fifty per cent of the difficulty of memorization for the speaker.

The qualities essential to good arrangement are unity, order, proportion, and progress. There must be one sermon, not two or more disconnected messages given as one. Each part of the material must be in its right location, proportion and connections.

John Dixon[3] says that for purposes of clarity the arrangement must provide for unity, coherence, simplicity, directness, and conciseness.

The arrangement of material is usually indicated by points or divisions. Out of a sound proposition, with its key word and transitional sentence, should come a series of main points and sub-points, clearly marking the progress of thought and rightly arranging the material in that line of thought Therefore, we must turn to the consideration of points or divisions.

VARY YOUR PRINCIPLES OF DIVISION

The principle of division aids us in formulating and arranging the main points. Only one principle of division should be used in any given sermon. To use more than one principle of division results in confusion and disorder, such as mixing reasons and methods, causes and results, or motives and goals.

[2] *Quarterly Journal of Speech*, Vol. XIV, Feb., 1928, p. 45.
[3] John Dixon, *How to Speak* (Abingdon-Cokesbury, New York, 1949), p. 7.

The proposition is the statement of the sermon in one sentence, the sermon in a nutshell. All the main points should flow out of the proposition, because they are inherently contained in it. Sub-points should be logically arranged under each respective main point and vitally related to it in the same way that main points are related to the proposition.

We now consider the main principles of division which may be used to seek good arrangement:

1. *Chronological,* when we arrange the points in time-order, as in narrating events.

2. *Geographical,* when the points are arranged according to an orderly directional sequence, such as from east to west or north to south.

3. *Quantitative,* when the main points refer to items of differing sizes or amounts from small to large or vice versa.

4. *Deductive,* proceeding in main points from a general truth to specific instances.

5. *Inductive,* when the main points take us from specific cases to the general truth they teach.

6. *Classification,* when the points classify truths or objects according to a system, such as the monetary.

7. *Psychological,* such as Alan Monroe's motivated sequence, when we follow the five-step outline in persuasive speeches. He says we first take the *attention* step, making the audience wish to listen; then the *need* step, creating the idea that this is the thing to do, believe, or

feel to satisfy the need; then the *satisfaction* step which seeks to get the audience to agree that your proposal is correct; then comes the *visualization* step, when we cause the listener to picture himself enjoying the satisfaction of doing, believing, or feeling this action; and, finally, comes the *action* step, when we ask the hearer to do, believe, accept, or feel what we present.[4]

8. *Cause and effect or vice versa,* when we proceed from a cause to its effects, or from the effects to the cause.

9. *Similarity,* showing the respects in which one thing is similar to another. We often use this principle of division when preaching on the types, or in developing analogous relationships.

10. *Dissimilarity,* showing the differences or superiorities of one thing to another.

11. *Negation,* when we show that a thing is not this, not that, nor the other. In the conclusion is given the positive answer.

12. *Partitional,* when we divide anything into its constituent or logical parts.

13. *Problem solving,* when we lay down a problem and suggest various solutions to it, all leading us up to the final and best one.

14. The *process method,*[5] in which the points

[4] Alan Monroe, *Principles and Types of Speech,* p. 201.
[5] James W. Armstrong, *Public Speaking for Everyone* (Harper and Brothers, New York, 1947), Part III, pp. 81–85.

deal with a series of actions by which something is made or done, so that the process is followed naturally from beginning to end.

Whatever the principle of division is, it should be closely followed, and enough points developed to give a fully rounded discussion of the proposition. Phelps says the divisions should develop the proposition. The divisions should be mutually exclusive. Each division should stand alone and not repeat or overlap other divisions, but should be vitally related to them. The principle of division governs the order and nature of the points.

VARY THE CONSTRUCTION OF MAIN POINTS

After the points have been determined they will need to be phrased for the best effect. An outline is always better if there is *parallel structure*. Sometimes one word will do for each point. When this is possible, then no point should have more than one word. Or each point may be indicated by a phrase, or cue, rather than by a single word or sentence. At other times, the main points may be given as statements or affirmations, sometimes as questions, or as commands, or as exhortations.

An exception to this is the *expanding outline*, which builds from a short point to longer and longer ones each time, until the final point is a full statement of the truth.

Alliteration, rhyme, alphabetical and acrostic

arrangement of points are valuable as memory aids, and often can be used, but a preacher should not habitually use any such device. If we have to twist the meaning of points, or break their natural order, to attain alliteration, rhyme, alphabetical arrangement or an acrostic, then we should avoid these devices. It is never wise to have an outline that seems heavy, stiff, mechanical, artificial, or smart. Breed says that the divisions of a sermon should be comprehensive, co-ordinate, flowing, distinct, unconventional, and original. We would say that the outline, as a whole, should be natural, symmetrical, strong, suggestive, vivid, and fresh.

VARY THE NUMBER OF MAIN POINTS

The *two-point plan* lends itself to presenting two contrasting truths, or the negative and positive aspects. Frederick W. Robertson was a master in using this plan.

The *three-point plan* Dr. Blackwood[6] calls the conventional pattern because it is used more often than any other. Three points seem to be just enough and not too many to most preachers. Alexander Maclaren often used this plan.

The *four-point plan* is suggestive of a four-square arrangement, and is frequently used by men like Clarence E. Macartney and James S. Stewart. The *five-point plan* sometimes will be necessary for the full development of a proposition. Robert E. Speer and William M. Clow sometimes followed this pattern. The

---

[6] A. W. Blackwood, *The Preparation of Sermons* (Abingdon-Cokesbury, New York, 1948), Chapter XII.

six-point plan also is mentioned by Dr. Blackwood. Some men use the *seven-point plan,* possibly with the thought that seven is the Scriptural number for completeness. However, we recommend a minimum of two and a maximum of five main points.

VARY THE METHODS OF DEVELOPING THE MAIN POINTS INTO SUB-POINTS

1. *Development by interrogation.*

We may apply one interrogative word to the main point and derive a series of sub-points, all answering to this one interrogative.

2. *Development by exposition.*

This process aims at making clear or expounding the main point. The following procedures may be followed under this method:

(1) Exposition by definition. In this process one strives to be accurate in explanation and also so to adjust one's meaning that the points will be unmistakable. There are various means of definition:

(a) by synonyms, words having the same or nearly the same meaning.

(b) by classification of a subject. These classifications may be chronological, scholastic, volitional, financial, affiliative, positional.

(c) by etymology, a study of the root meanings involved in the main points.

(d) by negation, telling what the main point is not.

(e) by illustration, chiefly by instances or examples, real or hypothetical.

(f) by context, identifying an item in its surroundings.

(2) Exposition by illustration.

(a) by metaphor or simile

(b) by figurative analogy

(c) by story (anecdote, fable, parable)

(3) Exposition by example. Aristotle recommended one example per point. There are several types of examples:

(a) reference to an event, situation, place, person, or thing

(b) general examples

(c) specific examples

(d) hypothetical examples

(4) Exposition by narration. This is the process of telling or presenting a series of events in story form. It is an elaboration of the context.

(5) Exposition by description. Here we put into word-picture form persons or objects, to tell how persons or things look, feel, or act.

3. *Development by argumentation*

The process of argumentation is called proof. The three rhetorical methods of proof are the logical, the emotional, and the ethical.

(1) Logical proof.

(a) The method of induction, the process by which we recognize a principle from the examples of its operation.

(b) The method of deduction, the application of a known principle to specific cases.

In carrying out these methods of logical proof, we will make use of examples, illustrations, testimonies, and statistics.

(2) Emotional proof. In persuasive speaking the preacher uses emotional materials in order to motivate the thinking, feeling, and conduct of his audience.

(a) Human interest material

(b) Humor for the relief of tension in both speaker and audience

(c) Animation and alertness in speaking in order to increase the attentiveness and responsiveness of the listeners

(d) Reveal by bodily action and words your personal interest in and concern for the issues presented.

(3) Ethical proof. This refers to the impression made on the audience by the speaker's intelligence, character, sincerity, and good will. It is always present and will be exerted by the speaker for good or ill, whether he is conscious of it or not.

In the process of exposition and argumentation two principles apply to the use of the forms of support. One is restatement. This is reiteration of the form of support in other language or in the same language. Another is the principle of cumulation, the use of any one form of support in series in the development or defense of any one point.

4. *Development by persuasion*

This is the process of moving the will. Dr. Alan Monroe of Purdue University sets forth in his book, *Principles and Types of Speech,* the psychological approach to a speech outline. He terms this outline "The Motivated Sequence," as referred to on pages 29–130. It is felt by the authors that the five steps noted in this sequence might well be used for the development of a main point, with a view toward moving the will of the listener.

The problem solving method proposed by John Dewey also may be used in the persuasive development of main points. This involves (1) the feeling of a difficulty, (2) discovering the difficulty, (3) a study of the solutions proposed for the alleviation of the difficulty, and (4) the discarding of all except the workable solution.

5. *Development by thought categorization*

This involves development by application of the general categories of thought. Dr. A. E. Garvie[7] believes that these general categories used in thinking can be profitably applied as guides in homiletical development. Some examples of these are:

(1) If the main point is an abstract idea, it may be illustrated by concrete instances, taken from Scripture, history, biography, or general literary works.

---

[7] Alfred Ernest Garvie, *The Christian Preacher* (Charles Scribner's Sons, New York, 1921), pp. 432–435.

(2)   If the main point involves a personality, this person may be sketched as to heredity, environment, development, capacity, character, career, achievement, and reputation.

(3)   If the main point is an event, this may be examined with regard to time, place, antecedents, consequences, human participation, and evidences of divine providence.

(4)   If the main point is a moral quality of an action, it may be judged as to motive, method, manner, intention, and results.

(5)   If the main point is a vice or virtue, it may be analyzed psychologically as to its origin, manifestations, and results from within the character as it unfolds in personality.

(6)   If the main point involves relationships, these relations may be itemized, e.g., love in relation to self, neighbor, and God.

(7)   The time order may be applied to the main point, showing its relationship to the past, the present, and the future.

(8)   The category of thought, word, and deed may be applied to some points.

(9)   The category of source, nature and effect may be used.

(10)   The category of a Biblical miracle of healing may be the case, the cure, the confession, the consequences.

(11)   The category of size or dimensions involves breadth, length, depth, and height.

(12)   The category of social relationships involves

husbands and wives, children and parents, servants and masters,

(13)   A category may show the spiritual status, such as saints and sinners, or preconversion and postconvention, or lost, carnal, and spiritual.

(14)   The spiritual progress category might involve call, commission, conduct, and compensation.

VARY THE METHODS OF ANNOUNCING YOUR POINTS

The old method, and perhaps the one most often used, is to announce the main divisions by "firstly," "secondly," and "thirdly," etc. There is nothing wrong about these terms, but they should not be used all the time. One can say, "My first point is," or simply, "first." Dr. George W. Truett used to introduce each division after the first one by saying, "And again we see that . . ." We can also say "further" or "Our next thought is," or "Note again that," or "We suggest in the next place," "Once more."

Main points should be announced so that they will be perceptible and not missed by the audience. There is no merit in hiding the main points but subpoints should usually not be announced. The transition from one subpoint to another can be in the preacher's outline and in his mind, but not be called to the attention of the audience. To do so will tend to confuse the subpoints with the main points in the minds of the auditors.

In cases of difficult material, one can announce all of his main divisions in advance and then repeat each as he proceeds. Recapitulation of all preceding main points is good, but this should not be an invariable habit.

REFERENCES

Homiletics

Broadus, John A., *A Treatise on the Preparation and Delivery of Sermons*. New York, London: Harper & Brothers, 1944, Part II, Chapter 1.

Garvie, Alfred Ernest, *The Christian Preacher*. New York: Charles Scribner's Sons, 1921, Part III.

Hogue, Wilson T., *Homiletics and Pastoral Theology*. Winona Lake, Indiana: Free Methodist Publishing House, 1949, Chapters 11–13.

Hoppin, James M., *Homiletics*. New York: Dodd, Mead and Company, 1881, Division 4, Section 17.

Reu, M., *Homiletics. A Manual of the Theory and Practice of Preaching*. Minneapolis: Augsburg Publishing House, 1950, Chapter 17.

Speech

Armstrong, James W. *Public Speaking for Everyone*. New York: Harper & Brothers, 1947, Part III.

Baird, C., and Knower, F. H., *An Introduction to General Speech*. New York: McGraw-Hill, 1949, Chapters 6 and 8.

Monroe, Alan Houston, *Principles and Types of Speech*. New York: Scott-Foresman and Company, 1939, Chapter 12.

Oliver, Robert T., Dickey, Dallas C., and Zelko, Harold P., *Communicative Speech*. New York: The Dryden Press, 1949, Chapter 4.

IX

Vary the Conclusions of Your Sermons

If a safe landing is the most important part of an airplane trip, the harvest the most important part of farming, the concluding chapter the most important part of a book, we may also say that the conclusion is the most important part of a sermon.

The preacher should have his objective or goal for his sermon in mind from the very beginning. As the gunner sights his gun, and as the traveler plans his journey's end, so the preacher should fix his objective for each sermon.

VARY THE PURPOSE OF CONCLUSIONS

The conclusion does not merely end the sermon, nor restate its purpose, but attempts to fix that purpose indelibly in the mind and conscience of the hearers so that right action will be forthcoming.

Your conclusion may include one or more of the following purposes:

1. To summarize the main ideas and to refresh the mind of the audience concerning them;

2. To tie the loose ends together, and make the unity of the sermon fully evident;

3. To rivet the truth in the hearers' memory with a final blow;

4. To commit the vital and eternal issues of the sermon to the decision of the hearers; to secure a verdict;

5. To show ways and means of using the truth preached; suggest a course of action;

6. To bring everything into a burning focus of personal encounter with the daily life of the listener;

7. To appeal for the acceptance of a new belief, or a correction of present beliefs;

8. To indicate a happy and desirable contrast to severe truth; e.g., one may be preaching on sin, judgment, or eternal punishment and wish to offset it by an appeal to righteousness, faith, or heaven.

ERRORS TO AVOID IN CONCLUSIONS

1. Avoid letting interest lag in the conclusion. Hold sufficient material and force in reserve to make the conclusion an effective climax.

2. Avoid making the conclusion too long. It should be brief and pointed.

3. Avoid giving the impression that you are about to conclude, when you are not. Sometimes preachers reach several good concluding points before they finally stop. Dr. Charles R. Brown points out that the preacher

should not be like a crow circling and circling over a rail fence trying to decide on which rail to light.

4. Avoid introducing new material not pertinent to the theme. Dr. G. Campbell Morgan says that the conclusion should conclude the sermon, preclude new material, and include a proper summary and application of the message.

5. Avoid concluding a serious message with a joke or humorous remark. One preacher closed with such a remark, "And, now as the little dog, with the end of his tail in his mouth, said, 'That's the end of me.'"

6. Avoid monotony in conclusions. Do not conclude the same way every time. The surprise element and variety in conclusions will help you to achieve your purpose.

7. Avoid trite, hackneyed conclusions. These are indicated by such expressions as, "Now, in conclusion, we see," or "Let us apply these truths to our daily lives," or "Let us all try to live closer to the Lord." When a preacher has not properly prepared his conclusion, he will probably fall back on commonplace, general exhortations.

8. Avoid apologizing in the conclusion. If you apologize you will likely call attention to something that many of your hearers have not seen or do not know. When a preacher apologizes he mistakenly infers that the congregation considers him of more importance than his message.

9. Avoid a formal announcement of your conclusion. If it has been carefully prepared, it will not need any introductory remarks.

DESIRABLE CHARACTERISTICS OF CONCLUSIONS

1. Brevity		11. Appropriateness
2. Clarity		12. Naturalness
3. Correct phrasing		13. Personal application
4. Intensity		14. Positiveness
5. Freshness		15. Distinctness
6. Variety		16. Impressiveness
7. Well prepared		17. Persuasiveness
8. Vigor		18. Effectiveness
9. Climax		19. Striking
10. Practicality		20. Eloquent

The conclusion should be so carefully prepared and phrased that it will prove itself to be the specific conclusion for that particular sermon.

VARY THE TYPES OF CONCLUSIONS[1]

Conclusions fall into four general types with several subtypes.

1. The recapitulation conclusion:
   (1) The formal summary, in which the main points are repeated without changing their terminology;
   (2) The paraphrased summary, in which the main points are repeated in words arousing new interests;
   (3) The common sense summary, in which the main points are rephrased in the words of the man of the street;

---

[1] Sarett and Foster, *Basic Principles of Speech*, p. 510–521.

(4) The epigrammatic summary, in which the main points are reduced to a single word for each point, e.g., stop, look, listen;

2. The application conclusion:

(1) In which ways and means of making the application are suggested;

(2) In which the application is focalized sharply on the daily life;

3. The motivation conclusion:

(1) In which the message is related to matters of personal interest;

(2) In which the appeal is made to lofty incentives;

4. The contrast conclusion:

The contrast conclusion in which hopeful, comforting, or inspiring thoughts are set in contrast to severe truths;

5. The anticipatory conclusion:

In which objections are foreseen and answered.

VARY THE INSTRUMENTS USED IN FORMULATING CONCLUSIONS

A conclusion may include one or more of the following instruments:

(1) A restatement of the text; (2) An apt quotation; (3) A fitting poem; (4) An earnest exhortation; (5) A story, or illustration; (6) An appeal to the imagination; (7) A contrasting truth; (8) A prayer; (9) An answer to objections; (10) A call for public response, a challenge,

a dare; (11) A rhetorical question; (12) An appreciation; (13) A proverb; (14) A promise; (15) A suggestion of ways and means; (16) A striking statement; (17) A parable; (18) A hymn.

If the audience knows a preacher's habit of concluding his sermons, they are mentally prepared either to resist his appeal or to ignore it. A generous use of the varied instruments suggested above will prevent this situation.

VARY THE MOODS IN WHICH CONCLUSIONS ARE PRESENTED

The conclusion is often the transition from the intellect to the heart, and should be composed in one's brightest moments or moods. But moods in which the conclusion is given may vary.

1. The quiet mood is a favorite one for many preachers.

2. Others may conclude in a mood of overwhelming appeal.

3. The tender or comforting mood is often in order.

4. The contemplative mood may sometimes be used.

5. The worshipful or devotional mood is an appropriate setting for some conclusions.

6. The bright, joyful mood will suit in other cases.

7. The serious mood fits the conclusions of many sermons.

The following suggestions regarding appeals in the conclusion are given by Austin Phelps:[2]

1. They should be founded on the strongest materials of the sermon.

2. They should be aimed at feeling as distinct from convictions.

3. They should be in agreement with the vital facts of Christian duty.

4. They should be specific in their basis and aim.

5. They should be prepared and spoken under the sway of genuine feeling on the part of the speaker.

6. They should not be developed at great length.

7. They should possess unbounded versatility.[3]

8. They should be uttered without forewarning.

This chapter has sought to indicate the possibility of variety in conclusions by indicating varieties of purpose, varieties of types, varieties of instruments, and varieties of moods.

REFERENCES

Homiletics

Blackwood, Andrew Watterson. *The Fine Art of Preaching*. New York: The Macmillan Company, 1937, Chapter 9.

Brastow, Lewis O. *The Work of the Preacher*. Boston: The Pilgrim Press, 1914, Section IV, Chapter 5.

Broadus, John A. *A Treatise on the Preparation and De-*

---

[2] Austin Phelps, *The Theory of Preaching*, abridged and revised by F. D. Whitesell (Eerdmans, Grand Rapids, 1947), pp. 115-118.
[3] See F. D. Whitesell, *Sixty-five Ways to Give An Evangelistic Invitation* (Zondervan, Grand Rapids, 1945).

livery of Sermons. New York, London: Harper & Brothers, 1944, Part II, Chapter 4.

Burrell, David James. *The Sermon, Its Construction and Delivery.* New York: Fleming H. Revell Company, 1913, Part III, Chapter 3.

Phelps, Austin. *The Theory of Preaching.* London: Richard D. Dickinson, 1882, Lectures 32–39.

Speech

Armstrong, James W., *Public Speaking for Everyone.* New York: Harper & Brothers, 1947, Part VI.

Sarett, Lew and Foster, William Trufant, *Basic Principles of Speech.* Chicago: Houghton Mifflin Company, 1936, Chapter 20.

X

Vary Your Introductions

In the introduction, the preacher seeks to capture the interest of his audience. It should answer this question: "Why should this audience listen to me discuss this theme on this occasion?" In order to answer this query, the preacher should prepare the introduction so that it establishes an interrelationship connecting text, theme, speaker, audience, and occasion.

The speaker meets the listeners where they are in their thinking and seeks to unify their thinking around his theme so that they will be prepared to receive his proposition and its development. Phelps says:

The introduction, therefore, seeks to bring the audience mentally and sympathetically up to the same level as the preacher, so that what is in his mind and heart may be floated over to the minds and hearts of his hearers.[1]

A sermon must begin if it is to be delivered. That beginning should be the best possible one. Therefore, the importance of the introduction.

The introduction should be prepared last because the preacher will not know what he has to introduce until the rest of his sermon is complete. Since the intro-

[1] Austin Phelps, *The Theory of Preaching,* abridged and revised by F. D. Whitesell (Eerdmans, Grand Rapids, 1947), p. 46.

duction must rightly adjust theme, speaker, audience and the occasion to each other, it is evident that it must be fully and carefully prepared.

Even as variety is possible in the other parts of the sermon, so is it in the introduction.

VARY THE PURPOSES IN INTRODUCTIONS

The preacher should include one or more of several purposes in the introduction in order to give the sermon a good start.

1. To establish contact with the audience; to put the speaker on common ground with his listeners;

2. To arouse interest in the text or theme to be discussed by emphasizing its importance and clarifying its terms; or to set the stage for the discussion by giving preliminary information;

3. To remove prejudice against either the speaker or the theme;

4. To bring calmness to the audience;

5. To put the speaker at ease;

6. To adjust the message to the occasion by making the theme pertinent;

7. To remove the ignorance of the hearers;

8. To make the transition from the natural to the spiritual.

PHYSICAL FACTORS INVOLVED IN GAINING AND MAINTAINING ATTENTION DURING THE INTRODUCTION

If an audience does not give attention to a speaker, it will not appropriate his message. The following physical factors are included in getting the attention of an audience:

1. Get the audience into one closely knit group located in the same section of the auditorium. This is known as polarizing the audience.

2. If possible, be alone on the platform, thus creating one center of attention.

3. From a persuasion standpoint, see that the lighting is adequate for both speaker and audience.

4. Avoid too high a platform. Failure to observe this will cause drowsiness on the part of the hearers.

5. If the speaker is introduced, let the introduction be short and to the point.

6. Walk to the pulpit with quiet confidence and assurance.

7. Establish physical directness by looking at the people rather than at the physical features of the room.

8. See that the temperature of the room is so adjusted that it will not rise above or go below 68° during the service, else the audience will become uncomfortable.

9. Have proper ventilating arrangements made before speaking, in order to keep the audience comfortable and supplied with fresh air.

10. Avoid distracting mannerisms such as fumbling with a watch, adjusting the pulpit lamp, removing hymn books from the pulpit, or rearranging your Bible.

11. Guard against an overuse of gestures in the introduction. Give the impression that you have a reserve of power for the coming climax of the sermon.

12. Without perturbance, publicly recognize unforeseen distracting circumstances, and proceed with your message. This is better than trying to ignore them or speak above them.

13. Dress so as not to call attention to your clothes.

14. Counteract whispering and inattention when you walk to the pulpit by pausing a few moments before you begin speaking. If this annoyance occurs during the message, lower your voice instead of raising it, or else stop speaking altogether for a few moments.

DESIRABLE CHARACTERISTICS OF INTRODUCTIONS

(1) Brief. It should not occupy more than 5 per cent. to 15 per cent. of the speaking time, depending on circumstances. An old lady told John Owen, the Puritan preacher, that he was so long spreading the table that she lost her appetite for the meal, (2) Friendly, (3) Frank, (4) Sincere, (5) Clear, (6) Appropriate. Phelps says, "Don't let the introduction be a piece of dead timber nailed to a living tree," (7) Modest. It must not promise more than the sermon can deliver. A layman criticized his pastor thus: "You started out by laying the foundation for a skyscraper, but you built a chicken coop upon it," (8) Direct, (9) Interesting, (10) Simple, (11) Tactful, (12) Unified, (13) Purposeful, (14) Suggestive, (15) Varied, (16) Audience-centered, (17) Informal.

ERRORS TO AVOID IN INTRODUCTIONS

(1) Flattery, (2) Apologies, (3) Triteness, (4) Complexity, (5) Lengthiness, (6) Severity, (7) Disjointed-

ness, (8) Abstractness, (9) Self-importance, (10) Technicality, (11) False starts, (12) Dry details about the background of the text, (13) Speaking too softly, (14) Revealing too much of what is to follow, (15) Lack of variety, (16) Remoteness, (17) Eccentricity, (18) Irrelevant humor, (19) Deception, (20) Verbosity.

VARY THE INSTRUMENTS USED IN INTRODUCTIONS

Some of the appropriate instruments, or materials, for use in introduction are:

(1) A startling statement; (2) A challenging question, or series of questions; (3) A good quotation; (4) A witty, humorous or amusing incident; (5) An epigram; (6) A vivid word picture; (7) A concrete example, or illustration; (8) A definition; (9) A comparison; (10) A discovery; (11) A correction; (12) A concession; (13) A paradox; (14) A rhetorical question; (15) A statement of a problem; (16) A news item; (17) A reference to a cartoon; (18) An object lesson; (19) An announcement of something significant; (20) A proposal; (21) A personal observation; (22) A commendation; (23) A statement of the special importance of the theme; (24) A parable; (25) A conundrum, or riddle; (26) A comment on a homely or familiar matter; (27) A prediction or prophecy; (28) A poem; (29) A brief history of the theme; (30) A proverb; (31) A prayer; (32) A reference to a previous speaker; (33) A reference to a popular book; (34) A reference to a current event; (35) An incident from pastoral experience; (36) A reference to a special season.

We suggest that the preacher try to use one or more of these suggestions from time to time until he has developed the habit of varying his introductions.

An audience likes the surprise or suspense element. If listeners feel certain of what is coming, they are likely to be listless or inattentive; but when they realize that they may miss something important if they fail to heed the first paragraph, they will form the habit of being alert from the very beginning of the sermon.

HOW TO PREPARE INTRODUCTIONS

Find some word, phrase, or idea in the proposition needing definition, clarification, or amplification. This starting point will serve as the main subject of the approach sentence. The approach sentence is the opening sentence of the introduction and should be constructed in its entirety prior to sermon delivery. It summarizes what the preacher says prior to the announcement of his proposition. This sentence will be followed by a number of subdivisions indicating its development.

This procedure concerns preparation, but when the introduction is presented it may be preceded by an appropriate illustration, description, or observation. An example follows:

Introduction: Neglect always brings its penalties.
    1. In educational pursuits
    2. In cultural development
    3. In physical care of the body
    4. In economic affairs
Proposition: Neglect in the spiritual realm always brings its penalties.

THE PROCESS OF SERMON CONSTRUCTION

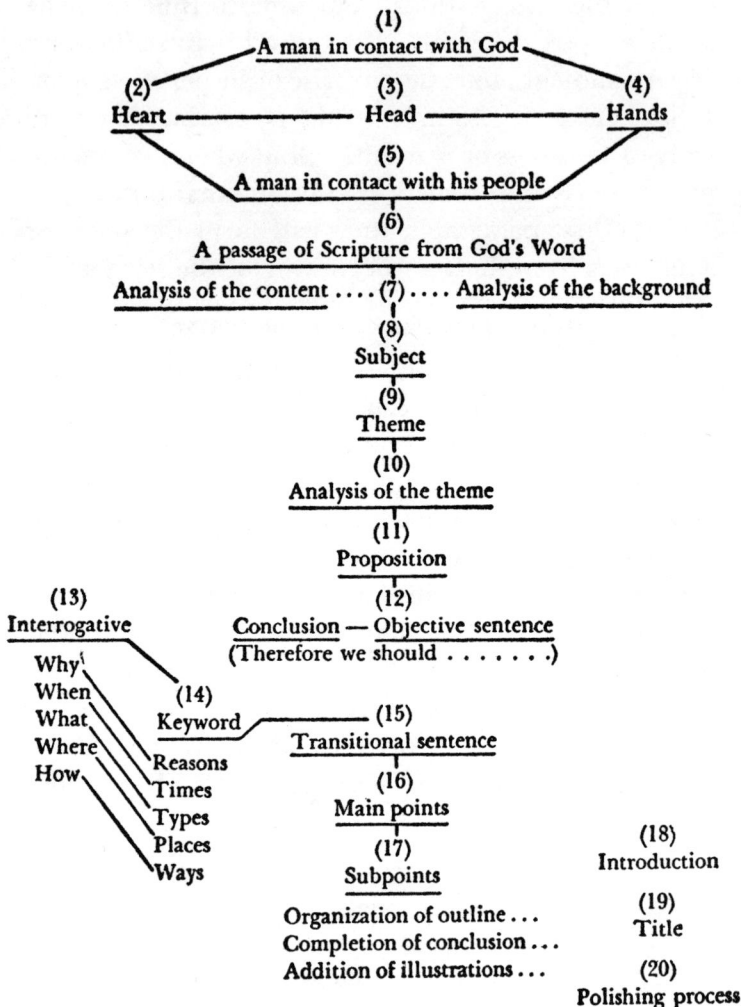

(1)
A man in contact with God

(2)   (3)   (4)
Heart ———— Head ———— Hands

(5)
A man in contact with his people

(6)
A passage of Scripture from God's Word

Analysis of the content . . . . (7) . . . . Analysis of the background

(8)
Subject

(9)
Theme

(10)
Analysis of the theme

(11)
Proposition

(13)
Interrogative

(12)
Conclusion — Objective sentence
(Therefore we should . . . .)

Why
When
What
Where
How

(14)
Keyword

(15)
Transitional sentence

Reasons
Times
Types
Places
Ways

(16)
Main points

(17)
Subpoints

(18)
Introduction

Organization of outline . . .
Completion of conclusion . . .
Addition of illustrations . . .

(19)
Title

(20)
Polishing process

If preaching a biographical sermon, or discussing a Bible narrative or event, the preacher may select the most dramatic or vivid part and begin with an imaginative portrayal of that. This arouses interest, and will enable him to introduce his character or event and state his proposition.

After the preacher has prepared his introduction, let him ask himself these questions: Is this material required for a clear understanding of my theme? Is this material so arranged that it will secure a fair consideration for my theme?

REFERENCES

Homiletics

Breed, David Riddle. *Preparing To Preach.* New York: George H. Doran Company, 1911, Part 1, Chapter 6.

Broadus, John A. *A Treatise on the Preparation and Delivery of Sermons.* New York, London: Harper & Brothers, 1944, Part II, Chapter 2.

Burrell, David James. *The Sermon, Its Construction and Delivery.* New York: Fleming H. Revell Company, 1913, Part III, Chapter 1.

Etter, J. W. *The Preacher and His Sermon.* Dayton, Ohio: United Brethren Publishing House, 1891, Part II, Chapter 8.

Hogue, Wilson T. *Homiletics and Pastoral Theology.* Winona Lake, Indiana: Free Methodist Publishing House, 1949, Chapters 7 and 8.

Pattison, T. Harwood, *The Making of the Sermon.* Philadelphia: The American Baptist Publication Society, 1898, Chapter 10.

Speech

Armstrong, James W. *Public Speaking for Everyone.* New York: Harper & Brothers, 1947, Part V.

Hayworth, Donald. *Introduction to Public Speaking.* New York: Ronald Press, 1941, Chapter 6.

Sarett, Lew and Foster, William Trufant. *Basic Principles of Speech.* Chicago: Houghton Mifflin Company, 1936, Chapter 16.

Williamson, Arleigh B., Fritz, Charles A. and Ross, Harold Raymond. *Speaking In Public,* New York: Prentice-Hall, Inc., 1948, Chapter 14.

XI

Vary the Methods of Presenting
Your Sermons

At first thought, it might seem that there is little or no variety possible in methods of presenting sermons. We believe, however, that a good measure of variety is possible here also when we consider the whole scope of a pastor's preaching responsibility.

VARY THE SETTINGS FOR REGULAR CHURCH SERVICES

We are thinking here of the Sunday morning and Sunday evening church services, and shall discuss them separately.

The Sunday morning church service. Since this service is usually more formal, dignified, and orderly, less variety of presentation can be realized, but there is some possibility even here.

(1) *Communion services.* The frequency of this service varies with different denominations, and with local churches within denominations, but it is quite frequently observed once a month, either morning or evening. Since the Lord's Supper is an object lesson presenting the central truths of the Gospel, the communion message should be merged somehow with the

administration of the Lord's Supper so that they form a unit. The themes will fit the communion service, and the pastor may wish to stand behind the communion table. The deacons may sit in their places alongside the pastor during the whole service rather than come up at the close.

Additional suggestions for varying this service can be found in such manuals as the *Cokesbury Communion Manual*, the *Star Book for Ministers*, *Minister's Service Book* by J. D. Morrison, and *Services for Special Occasions* by Martyn Summerbell.

(2) *Baptismal services.* These may be conducted in connection with either morning or evening services. Here, again, the message has a setting which should not be ignored. Baptism by immersion is a sermon in itself and the sermon should be in harmony with it.

(3) *Special seasonal services.* The annual days demanding special recognition can hardly be overlooked. Christmas and Easter are the two main ones. The church decorations will likely reflect the day. Christmas arrangements make the setting appropriate for a message on the incarnation or the first advent of Christ. The Easter day services will probably mean flowers, a baptismal service, larger audiences, and special Easter music, all providing a somewhat different setting for the Easter message which must not be crowded out Every part of the service must be keyed to the resurrection theme.

Thanksgiving Sunday may be the time for a Harvest Home celebration. Often the products of the field are on display in the church auditorium.

Other days commonly given recognition are Mother's Day, Children's Day, Father's Day, Labor Day, and Independence Day. All of them can become occasions for some changes, however slight, in the setting for the sermon.

The Sunday evening church service. Often the informality and adaptability of this service offers more possibility of variety for sermonic setting than the morning service. All we have said about the morning service may be applied, at least on occasions, to the Sunday evening service.

Other changes in setting for the Sunday evening sermon might be rearranged choir seating, or a change in choirs, or use of an extra volunteer choir. It is well to have a young people's choir, a children's choir, and an extra volunteer adult choir, plus quartet and special numbers for the Sunday evening service.

The use of lighting effects can provide variety of setting for the Sunday evening service. We need to take caution not to make the Sunday evening service too theatrical, but certainly some use of spotlights, flood lights, colored lights, dimming and shading of lights can be legitimately introduced. We must not use lighting effects to glamorize personalities, but rather to make the Gospel attractive. Variety, as we are discussing it in this book, is not considered an end in itself, but rather a means to bring more people to hear the preaching of the Word, and to make that preaching effective in more lives over a longer period of time.

Modern trends in persuasion through public address suggest that the auditorium be well lighted during the message and that light be concentrated over the speaker's rostrum.

We shall discuss the use of visual aids for the Sunday evening service in another section of this chapter.

Church anniversaries are observed more than formerly, particularly, 25th, 50th, 75th and 100th anniversaries of the founding of the church. Then there are recognition services in honor of members who have rendered outstanding service, or of groups attending in a body. Services recognizing young people going away to school, or to military service, or graduating from school are in order these days. Occasionally, some baccalaureate service or commencement service may be joined with regular church services. There will also be ordinations, receptions, and farewells for neighboring pastors. These always give a different setting for the sermon.

Funeral services. Here the setting is definitely prescribed, as well as the type of message. A pastor should seek to bring fresh, comforting, and brief funeral messages. Occasionally, a set of selected Scripture readings is desired instead of a message. This practice is becoming more common, but usually a message of twelve to fifteen minutes will be expected. Here is the place for Biblical messages, not eulogies of the deceased. The funeral sermon should not be evangelistic, though it should have an evangelistic note. Since most funerals are held in funeral homes or chapels, the setting is entirely different from that of the home church pulpit, but even when held in the church it is a special type of service.

A pastor is called on to preach in many types of services outside his own pulpit, and these provide a different setting and occasion for his messages. The pastor should adapt each message to its occasion. We shall consider some of these:

1. *Outdoor services.* A Sunday night service may be held on the lawn in good summer weather, or on the church roof if it is flat. Such services have a special usefulness in non-Protestant areas. Here a proper amplifying system, with the approval of the city authorities, will give the whole neighborhood a chance to listen to the services. What a setting for a warm-hearted evangelistic message!

2. There will often be union Sunday evening services during July and August in the park, the band shell, or a community auditorium.

3. *Institutional services.* The pastor will be asked to speak in jails, in hospital chapels, in old people's homes, in children's homes, and in state and county institutions. All these provide a different setting for direct, vital Gospel messages.

4. *Organizational messages.* Many calls come to speak before various organizations. These may range all the way from large conventions, to service clubs, family reunions, Parent Teachers' Associations, and

labor groups. Practically all will be meeting in their own accustomed places.

5. *School messages.* The pastor will have occasion to speak to the local high school assembly, to give college and seminary chapel addresses, and occasionally to speak in vocational schools of various types. The speaker needs to be alert, have interesting material, and speak within proper time limits on these occasions.

6. *Special outdoor messages.* In addition to all the services already discussed, there may be outside occasions, such as Easter sunrise services, Good Friday outdoor services, civic celebrations, Memorial Day services, and patriotic occasions at which the pastor may be called upon to speak or participate.

With such variety of services, the pastor will wish to be well prepared and properly adjusted to the occasion.

VARY THE METHODS OF COMMUNICATION

Most of the accepted audio-visual methods used in teaching can be adapted to preaching.

Dale's Ten Methods of Communicating Ideas. Edgar Dale's book on *Audio-Visual Methods in Teaching*[1] contains a most challenging chapter on the "Cone of Experience," which every preacher might well consider. This cone of experience classifies into ten categories the various teaching aids between the extremes of pure abstraction and direct experience. The author does not claim perfection for his classification, but his

[1] Edgar Dale, *Audio-Visual Methods in Teaching* (The Dryden Press, New York, 1946), Chapter 4.

diagram and discussion will impress any reader with the value of putting as much experiential material as possible into his methods of communication. Discussing it in inverse order to that of the book, we see that the method of communication by verbal symbols is the most elastic and comprehensive, and also the most difficult. Verbal symbols are words in the realm of absolute abstractness. While little children learn words and their meanings, the ideas communicated thereby are received with the most difficulty, and impressions remain the shortest time.

The next most difficult method of communication is that of visual symbols: charts, graphs, maps, etc. In descending order of difficulty to understand, the methods of communication in teaching are as follows: still pictures, radio and recordings, one-dimensional aids; motion pictures, in which the dimension of motion is added, but with the viewer only a spectator; exhibits, which one can view while operating or handling; field trips, in which the spectator sees and observes more than a picture or model (he sees the real thing as it is); demonstrations, in which the observer sees how certain things are done; dramatic participation, wherein the learner participates in a re-enactment of an event; contrived experiences, an editing of reality which makes it easier to grasp the reality by the study or use of the thing itself, as of machines, automobiles, airplanes; and the final tenth stage, in which full concreteness is achieved as in direct purposeful experience. Dale says that this is "the rich, full-bodied experience that is the bedrock of all education. It is the purposeful experience that is seen, handled, tasted, felt, touched, smelled."[2] This is learning by doing, as in apprenticeship. Dale has thus evaluated the communication methods used by the teacher.

If preachers are to make their sermons interesting, vital, and life-changing they should seek to communicate in the most concrete experiential ways. The following seven methods of communication are available to the preacher:

1. *The spoken word.* The preacher must rely largely on this vehicle, but he should do all he can to make his language concrete, vivid, picturesque, and colorful. By the right use of figures of speech, imagination and illustration he can achieve a high degree of communicability by this channel.

2. *Charts, graphs, and maps.* Often these can be used in connection with sermons, either presented on the screen from slides or in large size on a wall. Some Bible teachers have huge wall charts of Bible truth, the Biblical ages, and outlines of books of the Bible. Blackboard outlines, graphs and diagrams are possible sometimes. All these help to supplement the spoken word. While a pastor may not use them often, he can afford to use these aids from time to time.

3. *Still pictures.* There are some possibilities for this type of visual aid in preaching. One of the most common is the illustrated hymn lecture by the use of slides projected on a screen. There are many sets of slides on the life of Christ, the life of Paul, the patriarchs, the kings and the prophets of the Old Testament.

---

2 Edgar Dale, *idem.,* p. 38.

These should be used to supplement the sermon rather than to draw attention to themselves.

One of the authors preached on a Sunday evening on "The Blessings of the Clouds," having one of his men show colored photographs of cloud formations. The outline of the sermon was in the hands of the man at the projector, and he showed a different picture for each main point and each sub-point of the sermon outline. Kodachrome colored slides are very acceptable for this use. Other nature scenes, such as trees, mountains, oceans, rivers, fields, stars, animals, or birds, may be used to convey Biblical truths. By careful planning, about fifty slides can be used in a thirty-five minute message. This is a good way to use some of the men whose hobby is photography. Very life like three-dimensional pictures can now be used in this form of service.

4. *Motion pictures.* If these are silent pictures, they might possibly be used in connection with a sermon, but the timing would have to be worked out skilfully. Sound pictures would displace the sermon entirely unless they came before or after it. An increasing number of sound motion pictures are appearing, and most of them may be rented for an evening.

5. *Exhibits.* Under this heading would come models of the Tabernacle, the Temple, Noah's Ark, the Ark of the Covenant, the city of Jerusalem, or the land of Palestine. Missionaries usually bring home a number of curios which they use in their missionary messages. A pastor might well secure some such exhibits for some of his sermons

Field trips are hardly possible with a congregation, and neither are the other teaching methods Dr. Dale recommends. Dramatic participation is possible in church dramas and pageants but these should not displace the sermon. Contrived experience is hardly possible in a sermon, unless the preacher can so portray the life and experiences of a Bible character that the audience relives it with him. The final stage of direct, purposeful experience is what we seek to bring to pass in the life of the listener by our exhortations, appeals, and invitations for vital response to the Word of God.

6. *Object lessons.* We treat this method separately because it has such wide potentialities for pulpit use. Many ministers use the object lesson for children's sermons only to find that the adults are as much, if not more, interested and impressed than the children. There is virtually no limit to the number of objects that may be used. The preacher takes the object, a pencil, a baseball, a fan, into the pulpit and points out certain analogies between it and the truth he wishes to convey. Most religious book stores carry a number of books on object lessons. Any preacher can make his own, with a little thought and time. One minister lectures on "Vegetables I Have Met," using a number of vegetables as object lessons, comparing them to people.

7. *Varying the number of speakers.* Normally, a sermon is delivered by one speaker from beginning to end. He may quote and dramatize a number of other people in his message, but the spoken and heard sermon is all his own. We do not advocate any radical

changes in this procedure, but once in a while a minister might use one or more of his people to help give the message as suggested in the following paragraphs.

The dialogue is not too difficult to use. Two persons, using the question-and-answer method primarily, discuss the sermon theme in front of the audience. Or they might take different parts in reenacting a Bible scene. For example, the pastor might take the part of Jesus and a layman the part of Nicodemus in discussing the New Birth.

The panel discussion has become popular. McBurney and Hance write.

The panel discussion, which was originated by Professor Harry A. Overstreet, is a method of discussion in which a few persons (the panel) carry on a discussion in front of an audience, which usually participates later in a question-and-answer period.[3]

The panel discussion insures breadth, variety, spontaneity, and freedom, in contrast to the sermon or lecture, which insures order, compactness, and economy in presentation. If a panel discussion were substituted for a sermon, the members of the panel should be carefully chosen for orthodoxy, spirituality, and ability to communicate with the audience. The panel should be seated around a table in plain view of the audience, and, if necessary, a microphone should be available to each participant.

The symposium is akin to the panel discussion, but differs in that "two or more persons, under the di-

---

[3] James H. McBurney and Kenneth G. Hance, *The Principles and Methods of Discussion* (Harper & Brothers, New York, 1939), p. 288.

rection of a chairman, present in separate speeches the
various phases of a problem."[4] The audience participates vocally only in the questions and answers following the speeches. The purpose is to investigate a matter from several angles, not to present argumentative
speeches.

The forum lecture is the method by which a
speaker gives his message and the audience asks questions. It should not often be substituted for an evangelical sermon, but is a possibility.

VARY YOUR METHODS OF HOLDING ATTENTION

If the speaker can hold attention, he has a chance
to get a response. Mere silence is not attention, nor is
attention necessarily interest in the general subject.
Attention is positive mental application; it is active
listening. A minister cannot secure and hold attention
by merely demanding it.

One way to hold attention is to eliminate all the
things that may distract. Nothing unusual should be
on the pulpit, or near it, or even in the front of the
auditorium, to turn attention from the speaker. No
one should be walking in or out of the sanctuary. Windows should not be open so that people can see outside
the building. No sound or talking should come from
below or from the outside.

Positively, the speaker can hold attention by presenting fresh knowledge; by presenting what is novel,
exotic, or strange; by attacking principles, parties, men,
institutions; by giving the audience special "inside in-

[4] *Ibid.*, p. 299.

formation"; by dealing with common problems, as-
pirations, crises, temptations, defeats, and triumphs of
mankind; by carefully choosing his words; by using
effective pauses; by varying the rate of speed in speaking; by stressing important words; by maintaining eye
contact; by using proper gestures; by using visual aids;
by being as concrete as possible; by stimulating the curiosity of the audience in the opening parts of the sermon; by creating expectation and desire; by resting
the audience with proper illustrations and touches of
humor; by making visible progress toward the goal;
and finally by direct, personal application.

Dr. Bob Jones, Jr.,[5] suggests twelve ways for holding
the interest of an audience, namely, a carefully worded
title, the provision of rest periods every five to seven
minutes by the use of illustrations, the use of variety
in literary material, frequent changes in speech rate,
pitch, and intensity; the utilization of all four literary
types of discourse—exposition, argumentation, description, and narration; the direct quotation of other good
material, the introduction of something familiar, the
dramatization of ideas, the use of the unexpected, the
technique of suspense, the arrangement of points in
climactic order, and the provision for plenty of change
and movement.

Both the type of material and the method of presentation have a vital bearing on holding attention.

The sermon may be read from manuscript as J. H.
Jowett did, or memorized and recited as by the French

5 Bob Jones, Jr., *How to Improve Your Preaching* (Fleming H. Revell
Company, New York, 1945), Chapter VI, pp. 54-63.

court preachers, or absorbed and delivered extemporaneously as Spurgeon did. The extemporaneous method of delivery is widely recommended by the authorities on homiletics and speech. This is the method people expect from a Gospel preacher, a man with a message from God. We do not recommend any variation from the extemporaneous method of sermon delivery except for scholarly lectures or radio messages, when the preacher may be required to submit a manuscript. The extemporaneous method does not mean impromptu delivery or lack of preparation. Rather it presumes the most thorough preparation.

Delivery also concerns gestures and pulpit action. The preacher should stand erect, but not stiff, keeping behind or near the pulpit. His gestures should spring from inner impulses and should involve co-ordination of the whole body, not the hands alone. Good gestures have ease and vitality, are not cramped, are properly timed, are meaningful, are not overabundant, do not draw attention by extreme curves or extreme straight lines, and are not too abrupt.[6] Acts to avoid are twisting the body, glancing furtively toward the ceiling, floor or walls; twisting or tapping the feet, rubbing the body, snatching at the collar, clasping hands across the abdomen, swaying from side to side, shifting the body weight in an extreme manner from one hip to the other, standing tiptoe, leaning on the pulpit or lying across it, hammering the Bible with the fist, and racing back and forth across the platform like a caged lion. Dr. George M. Glasgow writes:

[6] Based on suggestions of Sarett and Foster, *Basic Principles of Speech*, pp. 181–186.

In all bodily movements the action should be positive and forward, not negative and backward. All movements should be purposive in intention and action. Resolution and conviction should always be present in the speaker's communicative attitude.[7]

The man of God should look directly into the eyes of his hearers, glancing from one to the other. His countenance should radiate Christian cheer and courage. He could well have someone posted to call his attention to awkward gestures and distracting habits in delivery since it is easy to fall into them unconsciously.

Delivery also concerns the *voice*. Since defects of gesture, speech, or voice may destroy some of the effectiveness of communication, it is necessary to use the voice in the best possible way.

In the use of the voice the preacher should strive for variety in volume, pitch, quality, and rate of delivery. The preacher should speak with sufficient loudness or volume to be heard easily by all auditors. He should be careful not to let his voice fade away at the end of sentences. The high-pitched voice is to be avoided, especially at the beginning of a message. The most common cause of the high-pitched voice is hypertension. As to quality, the voice should be mellow and resonant rather than harsh, nasal, or rasping. The maladjustment of the preacher in his home or church life will tend to destroy the pleasing quality of his voice. As for rate of delivery, the speaker should vary his rate of speaking. Tests have determined that a speaking rate of 115 to 140 words per minute is best for audience

[7] This quotation and some of the immediately preceding suggestions are taken from *Dynamic Public Speaking*, by George M. Glasgow (Harper & Brothers, New York, 1950), pp. 21, 30–34.

comprehension. Pausing and phrasing should be given adequate consideration. Every speaker should strive for clear articulation and should pronounce his words within the bounds of acceptability. These bounds will be determined by local, geographical, and sociological backgrounds.

Oliver, Cortright and Hager[8] warn against the following undesirable speech characteristics: nasality, throatiness, breathiness, raspiness, squeakiness, thinness, improper tone placement, monotone, recurrent pitch patterns, pitch too high or too low, unnatural inflection, volume too loud, too many pauses, stressing of unimportant points, excessive use of rate, pitch, volume, indistinct articulation, omissions of sounds and syllables, vowel interchanges, and consonant substitutions.

Delivery also involves style. A man's style is his characteristic manner of phrasing his thoughts, either in speech or writing. According to Broadus, its fundamental requirements are clarity, energy, and elegance. Phelps gives the essentials to a good style as purity, precision, perspicuity, energy, elegance, naturalness. The best style is that which calls no attention to itself. According to Dr. J. Oman, the defects of style resulting from overconsciousness of sound are the spacious style, the polished style, the fine style, and the flowery style. Rudolph Flesch, in *The Art of Plain Talk,* advises short sentences, with an average length of 11 to 17 words; the avoidance of too many words with suffixes

---

[8] Oliver, Cortright, and Hager, *The New Training for Effective Speech* (The Dryden Press, New York, 1946), p. 231.

and affixes, the use of many personal references; avoidance of long words, technical words, empty words like prepositions, conjunctions, connectives.

The modern emphasis in the speech field is on the conversational approach. The essentials of the conversational style are sincerity, straightforwardness, naturalness, alertness, respect for listeners, responsiveness to the moods of the audience, spontaneity, directness, freedom from inhibitions and artificiality. Oliver, Cortright and Hager summarize it this way:

The effective speaker will be (1) genuinely communicative; (2) direct; (3) animated; (4) vocally and physically free; (5) varied; (6) responsive to the moods and attitudes of his audience; and (7) a master of the personalized and intimate touch.[9]

As the preacher strives to employ these various methods of presentation, the following general suggestions may well be heeded: He should seek to be in good physical condition; he should keep his mind active while speaking; he should practice his material shortly before public presentation; and he should keep in the spirit of the material being presented.[10]

REFERENCES

Homiletics

Brastow, Lewis O. *The Work of the Preacher*. Boston: The Pilgrim Press, 1914, Section III, Chapter 5.

[9] Oliver, Cortright, and Hager, *idem.*, p. 129.
[10] These are a few of the suggestions included in the article entitled "Methods of Memorization for the Speaker and Reader," by Earl W. Wells, Vol. XIV, February 1928, *The Quarterly Journal of Speech*, pp. 39–64.

Etter, J. W. *The Preacher and His Sermon*. Dayton, Ohio: United Brethren Publishing House, 1891, Part III, Chapter 3.

Jordan, Gerald Ray. *You Can Preach*. New York: Fleming H. Revell Company, 1951, Chapter 17.

Liske, Thomas V. *Effective Preaching*. New York: The Macmillan Company, 1951, Part I; Part IV, Chapter 13.

Patton, Carl S. *The Preparation and Delivery of Sermons*. Chicago and New York: Willett, Clark & Company, 1938, Chapter 7.

Speech

Baird, C. and Knower, F. H. *An Introduction to General Speech*. New York: McGraw-Hill, 1949, Chapter 15.

Gilman, Wilbur E., Aly, Bower, and Reid, Loren D. *The Fundamentals of Speaking*. New York: The Macmillan Company, 1951, Part IV, Chapter 20.

Glasgow, George M. *Dynamic Public Speaking*. New York: Harper & Brothers, 1950, Chapter 2.

Norvelle, Lee and Smith, R. G. *Speaking Effectively*. New York: Green and Company, 1948, Part III, Chapters 11–13.

Oliver, Robert Tarbell. *The Psychology of Persuasive Speech*. New York: Longmans, 1942.

Oliver, Robert Tarbell, Cortright, R. L., and Hager, C. F. *The New Training for Effective Speach*. New York: Dryden Press, 1946, Chapters 6 and 13.

Oliver, Robert Tarbell, Dickey, Dallas C. and Zelko, Harold P., *Communicative Speech*. New York: The Dryden Press, 1949, Chapters 5 and 10.

Yeager, Willard Hayes. *Effective Speaking for Every Occasion*. New York: Prentice-Hall, 1940, Chapter 2.

For the preacher who wishes to obtain help in voice development the following books will prove useful:

Virgil A. Anderson, *Training the Speaking Voice* (Oxford University Press, New York, 1942).

James F. Bender and Victor A. Fields, *Principles and Practices of Speech Correction* (Crofts, New York, 1938).

Grant Fairbanks, *Voice and Articulation* drill book (Harper and Brothers, New York, 1940).

Victor Alexander Fields and James F. Bender, *Voice and Diction* (Macmillan Company, New York, 1949).

F. Holmes and D. Lincoln, *A Handbook of Voice and Diction* (Crofts, New York, 1946).

Harrison M. Karr, *Your Speaking Voice* (Griffith Patterson, Glendale, Calif., 1946).

Ruth B. Manser, *Speech Correction on the Contract Plan* (Prentice-Hall, New York, 1946).

C. Van Riper, *Speech Correction Principles and Methods*, revised edition (Prentice-Hall, New York, 1948).

Robert West, Lon Kennedy, and Ann Carr, *The Rehabilitation of Speech* (Harper and Brothers, New York, 1937).

If the preacher is interested in further study in public speaking he can consult:

Lionel Crocker, *Public Speaking for College Students* (American Book Company, Chicago, 1941).

C. Donald Bryand and K. R. Wallace, *Fundamentals of Public Speaking* (Appleton-Century Company, New York, 1947).

Gilman, Aly and Reid, *The Fundamentals of Speaking* (Macmillan Company, New York, 1951).

Alan H. Monroe, *Principles and Types of Speech* (Scott-Foresman and Company, New York, 1939).

Sarett and Foster, *Basic Principles of Speech* (Houghton Mifflin Company, Chicago, 1936).

If the preacher feels he needs help in the public reading of the Scriptures he should consult the following authorities regarding oral interpretation of literature:

Crocker and Eich, *Oral Reading* (Prentice-Hall, New York, 1947).

Jane Herendeen, *Speech Quality and Interpretation* (Harper & Brothers, New York, 1946).

Charlotte I. Lee, *Oral Interpretation* (Houghton Mifflin Company, New York, 1952).

Margaret P. McLean, *Oral Interpretation of Forms of Literature* (Dutton, New York, 1936).

W. M. Parrish, *Reading Aloud* (Nelson & Son, New York, 1941).

Woolbert and Nelson, *The Art of Interpretative Speech* (Croft, New York, 1940).

If the preacher has had no formal speech training, and desires a general introduction to the field, he should consult:

Avery, Dorsey and Sickels, *First Principles of Speech Training* (D. Appleton & Company, New York, 1928).

Baird and Knower, *An Introduction to General Speech* (McGraw-Hill, New York, 1949).

Borchers and Wise, *Modern Speech* (Harcourt-Brace, New York, 1949).

Gray and Wise, *The Bases of Speech* (Harper & Brothers, New York, 1946).

Thonssen and Gilkinson, *Basic Training in Speech* (Heath and Company, Boston, 1947).

XII

Vary Your Preaching Program

Preachers can easily fall into ruts in preaching, and, before they realize it, they are preaching one type of sermon most of the time, or are emphasizing a favorite doctrine to the exclusion of others. Every preacher should have a preaching program to avoid preaching from Sunday to Sunday on a hit-and-miss basis. Even though it be true that pulpit giants like Beecher and Spurgeon made their final decision on Saturday night as to their Sunday sermon themes, they were exceptions and not models in this respect. But these two pulpit geniuses kept a large number of sermon seed-thoughts in preparation all the time, and preached out of the fulness of extended reading, thinking, meditation, and prayer.

No aspect of sermonic preparation offers greater opportunity for variety than this part of the preaching task. Long-range planning can keep a man from repeating himself, and will enable him to feed his flock with a fully rounded pulpit fare.

The idea is to plan your preaching for weeks and months ahead, keeping a record of what you have preached in the past. This enables the preacher to cover a wide area of Biblical and practical material.

We can believe in and receive the aid of the Holy Spirit in working out a long-range plan for our sermons as much as we can believe in and receive His aid in preparing for the single sermon. There are definite values in planning a preaching program.

It saves time. We do not need to waste time thinking about what we are to preach. That already has been decided, and we can give our time to direct preparation on that predetermined theme We will not need to lose time hunting for sermon ideas. Adam Burnett writes:

Beware of that pernicious and miserable habit of wasting hour after precious hour hunting for a text, and being driven in the end to something that does not greatly warm the heart, or to plowing with someone else's heifers.[1]

It gives peace of mind. A preacher sleeps better and works better when he has his sermons planned weeks ahead. How disturbing and terrifying to have next Sunday bearing down on him and no sermons in mind!

It offsets interruptions. The unexpected is always upsetting the pastor's plans for thorough study and unhurried sermon preparation. Funerals, weddings, visitors, telephone calls, salesmen, conferences, all combine to nullify the best laid plans for finishing next Sunday's sermons. The man who has been preparing for several Sundays ahead does not mind these interruptions so much, for he already has his sermons well

[1] Adam Burnett, *Pleading with Men* (Fleming H. Revell Company, New York, 1935), p. 126.

under way and has enough material in sight to finish them quickly.

It drives the preacher to study. He has time to look ahead for the best material in his own library and to borrow or buy other books. With his material collected, he has motivation to read and master it leisurely. The preacher has no time clock to punch and can easily slip into laziness and slipshod habits if he does not map out a course of study big enough to challenge him to do his best. Planning one's preaching is a good safeguard against laziness and insufficient preparation. A. E. Garvie, principal of New College, Edinburgh, wrote:

There should be no need for hunting about for a text, or for waiting for a sudden impulse, or inspiration, as some preachers quite mistakenly call it. I have met with men who wasted more than half the week in a vain search, or as vain a waiting, for this inspiration, and then had to rush through their preparation of the sermon itself in the last days, or even day. The Spirit does illumine the mind in presenting often familiar words in a fresh light, but honest and earnest study is the necessary condition of genuine illumination.[2]

It inspires a teaching ministry. The best kind of preaching has a strong didactic element. Our Lord was a teacher as well as a preacher, and his Great Commission is clear on the command to teach (Matt. 28:19–20). Henry Sloan Coffin believes that the preacher must follow the teaching concept in his preaching. He writes:

[2] Quoted in *Thomasius Gospels Outlines,* by R. E. Golladay (Lutheran Book Concern, Columbus, Ohio, n.d.), p. 9.

A teacher plans a course of instruction; he does not select his subjects from day to day. . . . He asks himself what elements must enter into his teaching, what appreciations he must awaken, what information he must impart, what questions he must provoke, what purposes he must seek to instill.[3]

As a teacher prepares and follows a course of study, even so a preacher must plan to teach the fundamental doctrines of the Christian faith, the great ethical principles and moral responsibilities, the evangelistic and missionary motives and methods, the contributions of the Bible personages, the messages of the books of the Bible, the implications of the mountain-peak chapters, paragraphs, and texts of the Bible, and the prophetic forecasts as to the future. This requires a teaching ministry and a planned program. Dr. J. H. C. Fritz gives the Lutheran view of this matter when he writes:

It is, therefore, advisable that a preacher, at the very beginning of the new church year, make a program for his sermon work, a program which in the course of the church year will call for the pulpit treatment of every fundamental truth of the Scriptures.[4]

It makes for more timeliness. The man who looks ahead and plans his preaching to fit the seasons of the year, the special days, and the special emphases of the church calendar will have his preaching better adjusted than the man who does not. If something unforeseen arises demanding sermonic attention, the preacher with the planned program can turn aside

[3] Henry Sloan Coffin, *What to Preach* (George H. Doran, New York, 1926), p. 13.
[4] J. H. C. Fritz, *Pastoral Theology* (Concordia, St. Louis, 1932), p. 83.

easily, give the special sermon or even a series, and then come back to his program. When a preacher does not plan ahead, these special occasions may slip up on him so that he does not have time to prepare for them properly, or he may entirely overlook them.

Finally, it ensures variety. As variety is the major point of this book we put special emphasis on it. Principal Forsyth said, "We need to be defended from his [the preacher's] subjectivity, his excursions, his monotony, his limitations."[5] Dr. W. Graham Scroggie told the students of Spurgeon's College, London, that in his first pastorate he expounded the epistle to the Hebrews for thirty-two consecutive Sundays until his congregation became thin. The book of Hebrews certainly deserves serial preaching, but thirty-two consecutive sermons, without a break, is normally too much for any congregation, no matter how able the preacher.

The basic purpose of planning a preaching program is to include a wide variety of subjects, emphases, and types of sermons.

To summarize the values of planning a preaching program we have indicated that it saves time, it gives peace of mind, it offsets interruptions, it drives the preacher to study, it inspires a teaching ministry, it makes for timeliness, and it ensures variety.[6]

VARY THE TYPES OF SERMONS

Sermons may be classified under many arrangements. One already discussed is the expository, textual,

[5] P. T. Forsyth, *Positive Preaching and the Modern Mind*, p. 8.
[6] Many of these suggestions have been taken from the doctoral thesis of Rev. Roland E. Turnbull, Northern Baptist Theological Seminary, 1947, entitled, *Planning a Baptist Preaching Program*.

topical, determined by what one does with the passage
of Scripture under discussion.

Another variation depends on the kind and
amount of Biblical material used: sermons on Bible
characters, Bible types, Bible doctrines, Bible events,
Bible epochs, books of the Bible, chapters of the Bible,
paragraphs of the Bible, texts of the Bible, and words
of the Bible.

Broadus classifies sermons according to subjects
into four general types: doctrinal, morality, historical,
experimental, while Lewis O. Brastow classifies them
according to type of homiletic product as expository,
doctrinal, ethical, and evangelistic. And other classifications give us the hortatory, experiential, and occa-
sional types.

VARY THE PRINCIPLES FOR PLANNING YOUR
PREACHING PROGRAM

There are several principles one may follow, or
combine, in planning a preaching program.

The first is the principle of *the Christian year*.
According to this plan, the preacher bases his sermons
on Scriptures selected by liturgical leaders, passages de-
signed to fit the seasons of the year, and to emphasize
the basic Christian doctrines. The plan is used chiefly
by Roman Catholics, Anglicans, and Lutherans. Reu,
a Lutheran, says: "The Church Year is a miniature, as
it were, of the whole course of salvation compressed
into the frame of a single year."[7] And, on the same page,
he writes:

[7] M. Reu, *Homiletics* (Augsburg Publishing House, Minneapolis, 1950),
p. 328.

If we in the Lutheran Church did not have the Church Year with its festivals and its proper texts, we should be immeasurably less certain that we as Christians rest absolutely with all that we are and have upon the gracious doing of our God. . . .

The book of Scripture readings in the Christian Year is called a lectionary, while the reading for any given Sunday is called a pericope, coming from the Greek, *peri,* around, and *koptein,* to cut; and it originally meant an extract or selection from a book. The pericope, then, is a selected portion of Scripture consisting of a number of verses expressing a unity of thought which have been selected to fit certain Sundays and festival days of the Church Year, embracing especially the chief points in the history of redemption.

Each of the large liturgical groups today has its own system of pericopes adjusted to its own doctrinal and seasonal emphases. The pericoptic system can be traced back to about A.D. 600. The principle involved here is for the preacher to follow the system of pericopes for the year, deviating now and then as he may please but, in the main, holding to the assigned Scriptures for each Sunday of the year. The nonliturgical churches are not committed to the Christian Year, but some of its emphases might well be included in the preaching program of a Baptist, Methodist, or Presbyterian. Dr. Paul Scherer, a prominent contemporary Lutheran clergyman, commends this system in the following words:

For almost twenty-five years now I have done most of my morning preaching on the pericopes (or, as a printer once

suffered the word to stand, the "periscopes"!) . . . and I
have never felt them to be a hindrance or a slavery.[8]

George M. Gibson urges "a liberal use of the
Christian Year as a *guide* to worship — not as an authority over worship.[9]

Another principle of planning a preaching program is the *Biblical principle*. Here the thought is to
preach through the major books of the Bible in the
course of a pastorate. Some Bible books would be
treated in single messages, but others in a series of sermons. Variations of Biblical messages based on characters, events, doctrines, and texts would be mixed into
this program of preaching so that all the Bible would
be emphasized. Adaptations can be made to seasons,
special days, and unusual events. We favor this principle of varying one's preaching, as we believe it gives
all the advantages of all the others and yet holds strictly
to the Word of God.

The seasonal principle is another often followed.
Dr. A. W. Blackwood suggests a program for preaching
in which the season from September to Christmas is
the time of *undergirding,* with sermons on God in history and the great Christian doctrines; from Christmas
to Easter the emphasis is on *recruiting,* with Gospel
messages centering around the cross; from Easter to
Pentecost the aim is *instructing,* and the sermons concern the risen Lord, Bible ethics, and denominational
leaders; and the season from Pentecost to September

[8] Paul Scherer, *For We Have This Treasure* (Harper & Brothers, New
York, 1943), p. 160.
[9] George M. Gibson, *The Story of the Christian Year* (Abingdon-Cokesbury, Nashville, 1945).

is the time of *heartening*, with sermons on meeting life situations.[10] This principle is good but would tend to monotony if used year after year.

The *principle of discovering congregational needs* is good. Here a pastor surveys his congregation, by questionnaires, by careful pastoral visitation, and by studying his church statistics, until he knows the areas in which his people need development and growth. If the need is soul-winning, he gives frequent sermons and instruction along that line. If it is church attendance, or missionary giving, or Christian love, these are the themes which receive most emphasis in that year's preaching. One must be careful not to overdo one subject. Certainly a congregational diagnosis would point a pastor along helpful lines in his preaching program.

Another principle is that of *congregational suggestions*. The pastor asks the people to suggest themes, texts, doctrines, Bible characters, life problems on which they wish him to preach. He goes over these and bases his preaching on the suggestions most frequently made. We can see that this principle would be good to use in one period during a pastorate, but it could hardly be followed as a permanent planning principle, because the same problems and passages would tend to come up each time the poll was taken. Another objection to this principle as a permanent one is that people usually wish to hear their favorite doctrine or text expounded, and they need less instruction on that than they need on others in which they have little in-

10 A. W. Blackwood, *Planning a Year's Pulpit Work* (Abingdon-Cokesbury, New York, 1942), pp. 9–11.

terest. Prophetic students will wish to hear sermons on prophecy; those interested in the Holy Spirit will ask for sermons on that subject; and those who have loved ones recently taken to Heaven will wish sermons on Heaven. The need of these people may be for sermons on repentance, love, humility, self-sacrifice.

A popular principle is *to preach on trends of the times.* Some preachers follow the newspapers and magazines more than they follow the Bible. They are interested in preaching on current developments in religion, morals, politics, economics, education, athletics, and world affairs. Such preaching seeks to apply Christian truth to the developments of current life, and may be popularly received, but it does not develop people in systematic Bible knowledge and spiritual understanding. We believe that all preaching should be related to life and that our illustrations may be taken from current affairs, but the preacher is something more than a news commentator with a religious twist; he is God's spokesman set apart to declare, "Thus saith the Lord."

Another widely used principle is the *subjective.* There is no attempt here to follow any seasonal plan, or pericopic system, or Bible coverage goal, or to poll the congregation, or follow the trends of the times. The preacher preaches on what appeals to him as being the thing God wishes him to discuss. The principle is sometimes condemned as being too subjective — too much influenced by the preacher's hobbies and pet ideas. However, we can see that this principle is good if the preacher keeps in close touch with his people and spends much time in prayer for divine guidance.

These sermonic leadings from God may come at various times. They are recorded and preserved until such time as the Holy Spirit leads the preacher to select one for full sermonic development.

A final principle is somewhat akin to that of the Christian Year, but not identical. It is that of the *denominational program*. Most denominations adopt programs annually and seek to bring the pastors and churches into full support of the program. Sometimes they prepare a calendar of co-ordinated denominational activities and emphases which they mail out to all the pastors. These calendars give many useful suggestions for sermon themes. Most denominational programs include a period for evangelism, one for stewardship, and another for education, with additional suggestions for emphases on particular Sundays. Very few pastors follow out such denominational suggestions in full, but they can find helpful ideas in planning a preaching program.

We believe that by the use of one or more of these principles, any pastor can plan an intelligent, spiritual, Biblical preaching program for a whole year ahead, and continue to vary it from year to year over a long pastorate. By doing so he will help himself to be a better preacher, and will build up his people into well balanced, mature, discerning, Bible-believing Christians ready for every good work. We definitely favor the Biblical principle of seeking to preach in and through every book of the Bible in the course of a pastorate.

VARY YOUR SERMONIC SERIES AND COURSES

Any pastor can well afford to keep one sermon course or series going all the time. We follow Dr. A. W. Blackwood[11] in using the word course to indicate a group of sermons on the same general subject but without any connection between the sermons. A sermon series is a group of sermons on the same subject closely connected in consecutive order and in thought. A sermon series builds from one sermon to the next carrying the same ideas straight through in continuity and climax. In the series, the preacher announces the sermons as parts of a unified thematic whole, while in the course each sermon stands alone.

Once a preacher tries, he finds that it is easy to preach sermons in courses. He should not plan too long a course. Five sermons in a course is a popular number, seven is good, and ten is about the limit. People tire if a course runs too long, and a preacher inclines to repeat himself if he is not careful. The series is more difficult than the course because of its dominating theme, continuity, and climax.

Since the possibilities for sermon courses or series are almost limitless, a pastor can plan to preach from three to a dozen of them each year.

In order to make this chapter most useful, we are giving below a long list of titles for courses or series of sermons, realizing that each man will wish to rephrase the titles to suit himself, and to adjust the number of sermons to the needs of his congregation and his own capacity.

11 Dr. A. W. Blackwood, *Preaching from the Bible*, p. 41.

TITLE SUGGESTIONS FOR SERMON COURSES OR SERIES

These are listed below without regard to importance, chronology, or alphabetical arrangement.

1. The miracles of Jesus
2. The parables of Jesus
3. The personal evangelism cases of Jesus
4. The conversations of Jesus
5. The sermons of Jesus
6. The beatitudes of Jesus
7. The prayers of Jesus
8. Crises in the life of Christ
9. The Lord's Prayer
10. The Ten Commandments
11. A series on John 14
12. A series on Romans 8
13. Favorite Psalms
14. Nature Psalms
15. Penitential Psalms
16. Patriotic Psalms
17. Books of the Bible
18. Men of the Bible
19. Women of the Bible
20. Warriors of the Bible
21. Intercessors of the Bible
22. Backsliders of the Bible
23. Drunkards of the Bible
24. Apostates of the Bible
25. Men whom God killed
26. Men who wished to die and could not
27. Soul-winners of the Old Testament
28. Soul-winners of the New Testament
29. Conversions of the Old Testament
30. The Covenants of the Bible
31. The Feasts of Jehovah (Lev. 23)
32. Dreamers of the Old Testament
33. Men of Faith in the Old Testament
34. Men of Faith in the New Testament
35. Martyrs of the Old Testament

36. Martyrs of the New Testament
37. The Ten greatest miracles of the Old Testament
38. The Seven greatest men of the Old Testament
39. Missionaries of the Old Testament
40. Men called perfect in the Old Testament
41. The names of God in the Old Testament
42. The parables of the Old Testament
43. Procrastinators of the Bible
44. Singers of the Bible
45. Revivals of the Old Testament
46. Revivals of the New Testament
47. Great Sermons of the Old Testament
48. Theophanies of the Old Testament
49. Visions of the Old Testament
50. Visions of the New Testament
51. Vows of the Old Testament
52. Major types in the Old Testament
53. The ten greatest chapters in the Bible
54. The ten greatest prophetic chapters in the Bible
55. Great confessions of the Bible
56. Great decisions of the Bible
57. Men who disobeyed
58. Hypocrites of the Bible
59. Fools of the Bible
60. Major divine judgments of the Bible
61. Proud people of the Bible
62. Rebels against God
63. Self-righteous men of the Bible
64. Tempted people of the Bible
65. Worldly-minded men of the Bible
66. Major cities of the Bible

67. Night scenes of the Bible
68. Mountain scenes of the Bible
69. Major battles of the Bible
70. Lovers of the Bible
71. Questions Jesus asked
72. Questions the Father asked
73. Questions men asked Jesus
74. Lies of Satan
75. The development of the life of Christ
76. The development of the life of Paul
77. The development of the life of Peter
78. The Twelve Apostles
79. The Seven Churches of Asia Minor
80. Major doctrines of the Bible
81. Major aspects of Salvation
82. The Minor Prophets
83. The Major Prophets
84. Mothers of the Bible
85. The twelve sons of Jacob
86. The ministry of angels
87. The Tabernacle
88. The offerings of Leviticus
89. Great prophecies of the Atonement
90. Baptisms of the Bible
91. Paul's missionary journeys
92. Burials of the Bible
93. Offices of Christ
94. Major churches of the New Testament
95. Covetous people of the Bible
96. False religions of the Bible
97. Gardens of the Bible
98. Suicides of the Bible
99. Marriages of the Bible
100. The rewards of the Saint

In concluding this chapter and the book, we wish to suggest a preaching program for a three-year period. We have included a number of sermon courses and series of various types in order to show how these may be co-ordinated into a pastoral preaching program. The sermonic variety which we have been advocating will be found in the themes and titles of the messages included in this sample preaching program.

We trust that we have proved our thesis that variety should permeate preaching, but, beyond that, we hope that we have made clear and inviting the many ways to achieve diversity in preaching.

SUGGESTED PREACHING PROGRAM

First Year

Morning	SEPTEMBER	*Evening*

1st Sun. Vacation
Begin Series on Eight Greatest   *Begin biographical*
    Salvation Doctrines   *course on Genesis*

2d Sun. Depravity, total or   Adam, the first man
    partial?

3d Sun. The Atonement,   Noah, the perfect man
    God's answer

4th Sun. Justification, God's   Abraham, the pioneer of
    righteousness made   faith
    ours

OCTOBER

1st Sun. *Communion Mes-   Isaac, the well-digger
    sage, The power of
    divine fellowship,
    I John 1:7

2d Sun. Regeneration, God's   Esau, the carnal man
    life made ours

3d Sun. Adoption, God's   Jacob, the struggling
    family privileges   saint
    made ours

4th Sun. Sanctification, God's   Judah, ancestor of the
    holiness made ours   Messiah

NOVEMBER

1st Sun. Glorification, God's   Joseph, the fruitful
    glory made ours   bough
                      (end of course)

* Diversion from series

2d Sun.	Repentance and faith, what God requires (end of series)	The waiting harvest, John 4:35–38
	Begin course on the Gospel of John	*Begin series on Backsliders of the Bible*
3d Sun.	The eternal word incarnate, John 1:1–14	Lot, saved as by fire
4th Sun.	How to win men, John 1:35–51	Samson, ruled by his lusts
5th Sun.	Religious but not righteous, John 3:1–21	Naomi, turning back to idols

DECEMBER

1st Sun.	The water of life, John 4	Saul, deserted by God
2d Sun.	The two resurrections, John 5:19–29	David, the man after God's own heart
3d Sun.	*The Virgin Birth, a Basic Belief	*Christmas joy, Luke 2:8–14
4th Sun.	A New Year objective, Matt. 6:33	Solomon, the foolish wise man

JANUARY

1st Sun.	The bread of life, John 6	Jonah, the willful prophet
2d Sun.	Rivers of living water, John 7:37–39	Peter, from sand to rock
3d Sun.	The Light of the world, John 8	Judas, the son of perdition

* Diversion from course or series

4th Sun.	The light of the soul, John 9	Demas, lured by the world *(end of series)*
5th Sun.	The Good Shepherd, John 10	Is the world becoming better or worse? Matt. 13:24–43

FEBRUARY

Begin series on the Seven Greatest Books in the Bible

1st Sun.	The Resurrection and the life, John 11	Genesis, the book of beginnings
2d Sun.	A lesson in humility, John 13	Psalms, the book of heart throbs
3d Sun.	Comfort for Christians, John 14	Isaiah, the book of majestic prophecies
4th Sun.	Abiding in Christ, John 15	John, the book of salvation

MARCH

1st Sun.	The ministry of the Spirit, John 16	Romans, the book of theology
2d Sun.	The true Lord's Prayer, John 17	Hebrews, the book of better things
3d Sun.	Forward to the cross, John 18 and 19	Revelation, the book of completions *(end of series)*
4th Sun.	Up from the grave, John 20 (Easter)	The way of revival, 2 Chron. 7:14

APRIL

1st Sun.	Lovest thou me? John 21 *(end of course)*	The meaning of baptism

2d Sun.	The great commission, Matt. 28:18–20	The glory of grace, Eph. 2:1–10
3d Sun.	Christian certainties, I John 5:13–21	The two ways of salvation, Lk. 18:18–30
	Begin series on Major Christian Responsibilities	*Begin course on the Greatest Bible Texts*
4th Sun.	Prayer	Gen. 3:15, Warfare of the seeds
5th Sun.	Worship	Lev. 17:11, The power of the blood

MAY

1st Sun.	Bible study	Ruth 1:16–17, Destiny depending on decision
2d Sun.	*Eve, the mother of all	Isa. 1:18, Sins as scarlet
3d Sun.	Stewardship	Isa. 53:6, The sin-bearer
4th Sun.	Christian kindness	Daniel 5:27, weighed and wanting

JUNE

1st Sun.	Witnessing	Micah 6:8, What the Lord requires
2d Sun.	*David, a good father's failures	Habakkuk 2:4, Justified by faith
3d Sun.	Thanksgiving	Matt. 11:28–30, Rest for the burdened
4th Sun.	Growth (*end of series*)	Mark 8:36, The value of one soul

JULY

1st Sun.	The greatest freedom, John 8:31–36	John 3:16, The greatest text

* Diversion from series

2d Sun.	The blessed man, Psalm 1	Acts 4:12, None other name
3d Sun.	The Shepherd Psalm, Psa. 23	Rom. 8:28, All things for good
4th Sun.	Our refuge and strength, Psa. 46	Eph. 2:8–9, Saved by grace

AUGUST

1st Sun.	A prayer of penitence, Psa. 51	Gal. 2:20, Crucified with Christ
2d Sun.	Under His wings, Psa. 91	Heb. 7:25, Saved to the uttermost (*end of course*)
3d Sun.	Vacation	
4th Sun.	Vacation	
5th Sun.	Vacation	

Second Year

Morning	SEPTEMBER	*Evening*
1st Sun.	God warning the nations, Psa. 2	Souls at sea, Acts 27
2d Sun.	Missions, the primary task of the Church	Limiting God, Psa. 78:41
3d Sun.	Missionary equipment, Matt. 10:1–30	Prerequisites to soul-winning, Eph. 5
4th Sun.	Andrew, pointing toward Jesus	A song before the dawn, Acts 16

OCTOBER

Begin course on five minor prophets

1st Sun.	Hosea, the price of love	The motivation for missions, Acts 1:1–11

*Begin series in
Philippians on Blessings
in Bonds*

2d Sun.	Zechariah, the Lord remembers	Joy in prayer, Phil. 1:3–11
3d Sun.	Haggai, relative values	Continuing joy, Phil. 1:12–26
4th Sun.	Habakkuk, living by faith	Living in harmony, Phil. 2:1–13

November

1st Sun.	Amos: God's call to America (*end of course*)	Citizenship in Heaven's Colony, Phil. 3:17–21
2d Sun.	An abiding faith, Heb. 12:1–17	The challenge of a holy quest, Phil. 3:1–14
3d Sun.	The providence of God, Psa. 103 (Thanksgiving)	Living comfortably in a hard world, Phil. 4:4–20 (*end of series*)
4th Sun.	The tragedy of neglect, Heb. 2:1–4	God's ten per cent, Luke 17:17
5th Sun.	The dimensions of love, Eph. 3:14–21	Revelations in the rock, Isa. 26:4

December

1st Sun.	The challenge of His Name, Acts 3	Satisfaction guaranteed, Isa. 55
2d Sun.	The mystery of godliness, I Tim. 3:16	The value of a man, Psalm 8
3d Sun.	The Angels' song, Luke 2:13–15	Pageant

4th Sun.   The judgment seat   The swan song of a saint,
           of Christ, II Cor. 5:   II Tim. 4:6–8
           10

JANUARY

                                   Begin course from
                                   Gospel of John
1st Sun.   The year ahead,   The great discovery,
           Josh. 3:1–6   John 1:35–43
       Begin course on O. T.
           characters
2d Sun.   Caleb, a man with   The credentials of a
           another spirit   Christian, John 3:1–15
3d Sun.   Abraham, a friend   When blind eyes see,
           of God   John 9
4th Sun.   Joseph, true to his   The forsaken waterpot,
           trust   John 4

FEBRUARY

1st Sun.   Elijah, God's cure   Lights in the world,
           for discouragement   John 8:12
2d Sun.   Nehemiah, a builder   The New Testament
           for God   23rd Psalm, John 10
3d Sun.   Enoch, walking   God's bequest, John 14
           with God
4th Sun.   Daniel, piety in   The vital relationship,
           peril (*end of course*) John 15

MARCH

1st Sun.   A portrait of Christ,   The Lord's Prayer,
           Rev. 1   John 17
                                   (*end of course*)
2d Sun.   The hands of   The conquest of the
           Christ   cup, Luke 22:39–43

3d Sun.	The face of Christ	The crow of the coward, Luke 22:58–75
4th Sun.	The voice of Christ	The creed of the criminal, Luke 23:39–43
5th Sun.	The wonderful One, Isa. 9:6–7	The cry of the conqueror, John 19:28–30

APRIL

1st Sun.	Tears in the midst of triumph, Luke 19:29–48 (Palm Sunday)	The magnetism of the cross, John 12:20–32
2d Sun.	Revelations at the tomb, John 20	The missing member, John 20:19–28
3d Sun.	The resurrected life, Col. 3	Revival through the Word, II Chron. 34:14–28
4th Sun.	Living for Jesus, Col. 4	God's call for advance, Joshua 1:1–18

MAY

1st Sun.	The pre-eminence of Christ, Col. 1	Playing the fool, I Sam. 26:21
2d Sun.	Hannah, a godly mother	The mount of God's provision, Gen. 22:14 *Begin course on The Seven Churches*
3d Sun.	The secure union, Col. 2	Losing the first love, Rev. 2:1–7

| 4th Sun. | Burden bearers for the Lord, Num. 4:1–19 | Poor but rich, Rev. 2:8–11 |

JUNE

1st Sun.	Prosperity through obedience, Deut. 6	The danger of an unholy alliance, Rev. 2:12–17
2d Sun.	One-fault Eli, I Sam. 3:11–14	Condemned for tolerance, Rev. 2:18–29
3d Sun.	The profits of prayer, Job 1:1–16	The dying church, Rev. 3:1–6
4th Sun.	Is the young man safe? II Sam. 18	Living up to our opportunities, Rev. 3:7–13
5th Sun.	Life's disappointments, Exod. 15:22–27	An ecclesiastical failure, Rev. 3:14–22 (end of course)

JULY

Begin courses on nature sermons

1st Sun.	The life-giving voice, John 5:19–30	The message of the mountains
2d Sun.	Your logical service, Rom. 12:1–2	The message of the stars
3d Sun.	The Christian's assets, I Pet. 1:3–5	The message of the sea
4th Sun.	Why I believe in the Church	The message of the trees (end of course)

AUGUST

Vacation Month

Third Year

Morning	SEPTEMBER	*Evening*
1st Sun.	The mind of Christ, Phil. 2:5–11	Ripening and reaping, Matt. 13:36–43
2d Sun.	Delight in the Lord, Psa. 37:4	Praying always, Luke 18:1
3d Sun.	Divine rest, Matt. 11:28–30	Symphonic praying, Matt. 18:16–20
4th Sun.	The Power of Pentecost, Acts 2	Conversion, the false and the true, Matt. 7:13–27

OCTOBER

		Begin series on the Servant in the Gospel of Mark
1st Sun.	The work of the church	Preparing the servant, Mark 1:1–13
	Begin series on Sources of Spiritual Power	
2d Sun.	Power through confession	The servant seeking servants, Mark 1:16–20
3d Sun.	Power through surrender	The servant helping the helpless, Mark 1:21—2:12
4th Sun.	Power through Bible study	The servant facing criticism, Mark 2:15—3:6, 20–30

NOVEMBER

1st Sun.	Power through prayer	The servant teaching, Mark 4:1–34
2d Sun.	Power through the Holy Spirit	The servant winning victories, Mark 5

3d Sun.	Power through witnessing	The servant feeding the multitude, Mark 6:30–44
4th Sun.	Power through waiting and watching (*end of series*)	The servant commending a stranger, Mark 7:24–30
5th Sun.	Manpower shortage	The servant transfigured, Mark 8:38—9:13

DECEMBER

1st Sun.	A secret disciple (Joseph of Arimathea)	The servant questioning his questioners, Mark 12:13–37
2d Sun.	Radio station Y-O-U, Rom. 14:7	The servant foretells His glorious return, Mark 13
3d Sun.	Receiving God's Christmas gift, John 1:12	*The supreme beatitude, Acts 20:35
4th Sun.	Girding for the New Year, I Peter 1:13–16	The servant triumphs in the supreme test, Mark 14–16 (*end of course*)

JANUARY

1st Sun.	Love fulfilling the law, Matt. 2:38–39	Abraham's greatest trial, Gen. 22
2d Sun.	The profit of Godliness, I Tim. 4:7–8	Satan fallen from heaven, Luke 10:18
3d Sun.	Jesus' first sermon in His home church, Luke 4:16–30	A desirable dictatorship, Mark 7:2–27

* Diversion from series

4th Sun.	Forgiven and for- giving, Matt. 18:21–35	Satan's strongest ally (Intemperance)

FEBRUARY

		Begin course on the First Three Sons
1st Sun.	Christian patience, James 5:7–11	Adam's first son, Cain
2d Sun.	A plea for Jehovah's presence, Ex. 34	Adam's second son, Abel
3d Sun.	The soul-winner's shining, Dan. 12:3	Adam's third son, Seth
4th Sun.	Not by bread alone, Matt. 4:4	Launch out and let down, Luke 5:1–11

MARCH

	Begin course on Ephesians	*Begin series on Men Who Desired to Die*
1st Sun.	Blessed with all spiritual blessings, Eph. 1:1–14	Moses, distressed unto death
2d Sun.	Superknowledge, Eph. 1:15–23	Job, afflicted unto death
3d Sun.	Before and after, Eph. 2:1–10	Elijah, weary unto death
4th Sun.	The meaning of redemption, Eph. 2:11–22	Jonah, embarrassed unto death
5th Sun.	The divine mystery revealed, Eph. 3:1–13	Jeremiah, disappointed unto death (*end of series*)

April

1st Sun.	*Risen and ruling, Col. 3:1–4 (Easter)	The will of God, Acts 21:14
2d Sun.	A spirit-indited supplication, Eph. 3:14–21	Melchizedek, the mysterious
		Begin course on Exodus
3d Sun.	Walking worthily, Eph. 4:1–16	A star on the horizon, Ex. 1–2
4th Sun.	Walking differently, Eph. 4:17–32	The call and commission of a champion, Ex. 3–4

May

1st Sun.	Walking in love, Eph. 5:1–6	The challenge of a conqueror, Ex. 5–11
2d Sun.	Walking in light, Eph. 5:7–21	Striking off the shackles, Ex. 12–15
3d Sun.	Christianity in social relationships, Eph. 5:22—6:9	God caring for His own, Ex. 16–17
4th Sun.	The armor of God, Eph. 6:10–20 (*end of course*)	The thunders of Sinai, Ex. 19–20

June

1st Sun.	Daniel in the lions' den	Under the blood of the covenant, Ex. 24:1–11
2d Sun.	God's outlook on life, Mark 8:27–38	The truths in the tabernacle, Ex. 25–40
3d Sun.	A church at prayer, Acts 12	The golden calf condemned, Ex. 32 (*end of course*)

• Diversion from course

4th Sun. Faith accomplish-   Why does God allow
          ing the impossible,   war?
          Mark 11:12–25

JULY

Vacation Month

AUGUST

Begin course on
nature sermons

1st Sun. Does God help in   The message of the
          the minor details   flowers
          of life?

2d Sun.   Children and the   The message of the sun
          Kingdom,
          Matt. 18:1–14

3d Sun.   Strength for life's   The message of the
          strains,   rivers
          2 Cor. 4:16–18

4th Sun. Revival and   The message of the
          renewal,   clouds
          Joel 2:18–27   *(end of course)*

REFERENCES

Homiletics

Bailey, Ambrose, *Stand Up and Preach*, New York: Round
    Table Press, 1937.

Blackwood, Andrew Watterson, *Planning A Year's Pulpit
    Work*, New York, Nashville: Abingdon-Cokesbury
    Press, 1942.

Blackwood, Andrew Watterson, *Preaching From The Bible,* New York, Nashville: Abingdon-Cokesbury Press, 1941.

Blackwood, Andrew Watterson, *The Preparation of Sermons,* Nashville: Abingdon-Cokesbury Press, 1948.

Burrell, David James, *The Sermon, Its Construction and Delivery,* New York: Fleming H. Revell Company, 1913.

Donovan, Marcus, *Sermon Outlines for The Christian Year,* London: Mowbray, 1928.

Gibson, George M., *The Story of The Christian Year,* New York: Abingdon-Cokesbury, 1945.

Luccock, Halford, *In The Minister's Workshop,* New York: Abingdon, 1944.

Stidger, W. L., *Planning Your Preaching,* New York: Harper & Brothers, 1932.

Whitesell, F. D., *Basic New Testament Evangelism,* Grand Rapids: Zondervan, 1949, Appendix I.

Speech

Yeager, Willard Hayes, *Effective Speaking for Every Occasion,* New York: Prentice-Hall, 1940.

Index